Building A Successful Micro-Agency

A Guide To Starting Profitable & Sustainable Digital Marketing Agencies

Building A Successful Micro-Agency: A Guide to Starting
Profitable & Sustainable Digital Marketing Agencies
Copyright © 2022 Gil & Anya Gildner.
www.discosloth.com

ISBN 978-1-7337948-4-8

Published by Baltika Press

Printed in the United States of America.

GIL & ANYA GILDNER

Praise for *Building A Successful Micro-Agency*

"There is a longevity and stability to building a business the right way that is too often overlooked by the "SCALE IT TO THE MOON" crowd. In their latest book, Gil & Anya graciously open up their agency processes and philosophy to walk us through how they have managed and built their successful micro-agency. As a fellow "micro-agency" owner trying to do the same thing, this book is worth its weight in gold. The revolution of "stability over scaling" has begun, and Gil & Anya are leading the pack."

— Kirk Williams, owner of ZATO, author of *Stop the Scale: Building a Digital Agency You Actually Like*

Praise for *Becoming A Digital Marketer*

"Two marketers who know their subject well, and have the hands-on experience in the still-wild west of online marketing to know what works. They know what levers to pull. They advocate for an ethical, white hat approach, not quick tricks based on gaming the big gorillas."

— Gary Bengier, CFO of eBay

"Great content, and really well-written. If you need a resource for those learning PPC, this is the one."

— Rand Fishkin, founder of Moz & SparkToro

"The sort of content I wish I'd created."

— Steven Kenwright, co-founder of Rise at Seven

TABLE OF CONTENTS

INTRODUCTION

"All in all you're just another brick in the wall." - Pink Floyd, The Wall

If you are setting out to create the world's next Dentsu, Omnicom, or Publicis, you need to shut this book immediately. Not only is this book just not about creating a massive, full-service, billion-dollar agency...we have no idea how to do it, either.

If you have dreams of being the next Don Draper, you should just pitch this book into the nearest trash receptacle. Starting a business — *any* business — just because the niche sounds glamorous is a direct path to bankruptcy (and, let me assure you from years of experience, the world of digital marketing is the furthest thing from sexy).

However, if you're looking to build a solid, sustainable business in a growing field which will allow you to build a good brand, make a lucrative income, and become an authoritative expert in a particular domain, this book *is* for you.

Side note: this book is written from the perspective of Gil. Anything of practical value was probably contributed by Anya.

In March of 2017, thanks to a bottle of wine and a tiny bit of liquid courage, we decided to quit our jobs and start our own digital agency. In short order, we started creating our agency on the side. A few months in, Anya (who was my co-worker and girlfriend at the time) left to work on our agency full-time, and I handed in my three month's notice. By October of 2017, both of us were working full-time on Discosloth, which was by then making more revenue than we'd been making at our full-time nine-to-fives.

I will be totally transparent: we didn't know what we were getting into when we started Discosloth. If anything, we just knew what we *didn't* want to do. Truth be told, at the beginning I didn't have a whole lot of confidence that we could really make that much money running our own agency. I knew we could probably do okay, but I didn't have a lot of expectations beyond that. After all, agencies pop up left and right, all day, every day. Few agencies seem to last more than a year or two.

That was just over five years ago, and I have (thankfully) been proven very wrong.

In those five years, Anya and I have learned a lot about what makes up the bones of a good agency. I've met many agency founders who are really killing it — and learning from them has been a crucial building block in growing our agency. It's true that most startups fail (over a fifth of small businesses fail within the first year, and half of them will fail by year five).[1] But it's also true that it's entirely possible to succeed past your wildest dreams. It just takes some common sense, a lot of hard work, a keen awareness of what's going on in the world, an optimistic attitude, and perhaps a little bit of good fortune.

As I write this, Discosloth is a boutique paid search agency averaging between twenty and thirty clients on monthly retainer, including everything from local mom & pop stores to public Fortune 500 companies (we'll talk about client diversification later). Our revenue has grown an average of 40% year over year. Our roughest year in terms of growth was 2020, in which many advertising sectors were mandated to shut down, and in which the economy took a massive hit...yet, we were still able to increase our year-over-year revenue by 12%.

All of this has happened at Discosloth with just three full-time colleagues, and from time to time, a handful of contractors and consultants. This has let us operate at a profit margin of just over 82%. We've reached the point where, because of our brand building and our super-specific focus, we have a steady stream of inbound leads. We have the luxury of sorting through dozens of new inquiries each month, and pursuing relationships with those that are the absolute best fit for our agency. We're profitable enough that we've been able to establish the perks we wish we'd had back when *we* were employ-

---

[1] "In 2019, the failure rate of startups was around 90%. Research concludes 21.5% of startups fail within their first year, 30% in the second year, 50% in the fifth year, and 70% in their 10th year." - Investopedia, November 9th, 2020.

ees. Five weeks paid vacation, an annual bonus (an extra month of pay at the end of the year, also known as a "13th salary"), and an all-expenses-paid international retreat each year including spouses.

We started as a full-service digital marketing agency, doing just about everything under the sun that could make us money. We realized that was a short-sighted approach, so we swiftly narrowed down our portfolio of services to the things we did best: SEO, PPC, and analytics. After success in this focus, we then soon realized we needed to niche down even more. We cut out paid social, and stopped providing SEO as a service. Discosloth is now a hyper-focused paid search agency. The only three channels we work with are Google Ads, Microsoft Ads, and Amazon Ads.

Last year, I did some business consulting for a fellow who was starting up a digital agency in Los Angeles. He had found me through one of our previous books (*Becoming A Digital Marketer*) and reached out to ask if I was available for some startup consulting. He'd had a long career in niche logistics software sales, but finally wanted to branch out on his own.

At the end of our first call, he asked me what his chances were for success.

"Do you want me to be direct?" I asked.

"I'd better hear it now than later," he replied.

"If you want to start a full-service digital agency serving clients in your area, you have a 5% chance of success. You will almost certainly fail. There are millions of people out there trying to do the exact same thing."

He seemed a little crestfallen, but I continued. *"However...*if you create a niche agency for the logistics industry, focusing on one or two services you're familiar with like email marketing or paid search...you do have a chance of success. You're almost certain to get traction, especially since you've worked in this industry for decades and know lots of folks in it."

This holds true for anyone wanting to start an agency, and it's really the core central bit of advice I can give anyone.

If you want to create *just any* agency, you're doomed.

If you want to create a *specific* agency, you're gold.

My primary hope is that through this book, you will be able to learn how Discosloth was created, how other friends of mine in the industry have succeeded, and get an idea of how you, too, can create a thriving and scalable agency. It's important to note, however, that it is *not* the only way. There is no only way. This is merely what worked for us. Because we're so intimately attached to our own company, it's what we know best. Just because we did it one way doesn't mean it's the right way for you. We've definitely made some missteps, which other aspiring agency founders can hopefully learn from. But on the flip side, we've also made some really good calls which we think can be easily replicated.

My secondary hope is that I will be able to instill an important aspect into the minds of anyone who's looking to build an agency: the aspect of just *keeping on keeping on*.

A lot of folks want to start an agency. In the US alone, there are tens of thousands of agencies already in existence.[2]

Most of the new folks, unfortunately, see a few agencies become wildly successful, and this leads some to approach it like a get-rich-quick scheme.

Usually, these guys make a decent buck, and then become those statistics that close up shop after a year or two. Get-rich-quick never actually works in the long run, and the agency models that these guys create are totally unsustainable.

If you are looking to make a million bucks your first year, and cold call your way through ten thousand leads, churn through a few hundred clients, and act like a sales funnel pipelining all your production to freelancers or white-label agencies...this book is not for you. Close it immediately and return it, save your time and money!

If you're looking to spend the next five to ten years building up a solid agency with sustainable cashflow, decent clients, a good reputation, and the ability to weather ups and downs while making a respectable income, our sincere hope is that this *is* the book for you.

---

[2] "According to Census data, the number of establishments in the advertising and related industry in the United States has been oscillating at a little under 40 thousand since 2008." - Statista, November 29, 2021.

Chapter Takeaways

At the end of each chapter, we'll have a short section with take-aways. Usually these are questions you need to answer for your-self — and, of course, your future agency.

WHAT MAKES A SUCCESSFUL AGENCY?

"Don't think. Thinking is the enemy of creativity. It's self-conscious, and anything self-conscious is lousy. You can't try to do things. You simply must do things." - Ray Bradbury [3]

As the owner of your own agency, you get to decide what success looks like. And that's really the most important part about owning your own agency: it gives you independence to achieve whatever *you'd* like to achieve.

Maybe that's a certain number. $100k, or $1 million, or $10 million...doesn't really matter.

Maybe it's a lifestyle. 20 hours a week, 30 hours a week, 80 hours a week. Whatever you enjoy.

Or maybe it's the freedom. Traveling while working to various continents, or living off-grid, or living it up in a penthouse in New York City. There are many options!

As long as your numbers are in the black, and you're not losing

---

[3] Ray Bradbury, *The New York Times*

money, in my book you're doing well. There is no magic number, no magic win. All you really need? More money coming in than going out. As long as this always happens, and you're paying for whatever you want to achieve — lifestyle, independence, financial goals — your agency is more successful than not.

I've spoken to fellows who want to start their own agency, and they can typically be divided into two camps: the ones who will succeed, and the ones who will burn out. The successful ones have typically had some experience in marketing, want to do better work, and want to make better money. Simple goals, right? The unsuccessful ones tend to obsess about other things: "I want to grow this to a 100-employee agency" or "I want to be like Gary Vaynerchuk" or "I want to create 1,000 jobs" or "I want our agency to be a *family*."

Unfortunately, my very generous definition of success (simply pulling in more than you spend) is somehow still extremely rare. The simple goal of making more money than you spend is also quite hard to achieve, because there are so many challenging elements involved in this equation.

There is a basic, overarching path from A to B that every agency treads: taking possibility (leads) and slowly turning them into dollars (paying clients). In between A and B, however, the path isn't a straight shot. There are multiple steps.

The strategies and agency structure described in this book are not the *only* answer. It is *one* answer, which worked well for Discosloth, and which I think will work well for many others.

Our agency model looks like this: we built an extremely lean and efficient company with very low expenses, tightly focused on one specific technical vertical, and built up a brand over a few years which now provides us with a constant stream of inbound leads.

We avoid debt and extraneous overhead, and put our sights on positive cashflow that allows us to hire selectively, with a focus on quality rather than quantity. We would rather make more profit than revenue.

Our approach to profitability is based upon simplicity.

What does it take to get us from A to B, with the most simple, efficient, and dependable workflow possible — and *how can we have as few moving parts as possible?*

The path from A to B, which every agency treads, is never as simple as you'd like. In between getting a client lead and cashing in your paycheck, there are a lot of steps.

First, you have to *find* the leads.

Second, you need to *qualify* these leads to make sure they are a good fit for you (part of this is validating that they have money to give you).

Third, you have to *convince* them you're the best choice.

Fourth, you need to *fulfill* your promises and actually be their best choice, and show them how you *were* the best choice, and keep them around for next month.

And finally, you need to actually get *paid*.

Every agency founder will be naturally good in at least one of these functions...even if someone can't find client leads, they'll be able to fulfill the work. Even if someone can't deliver on the work, they'll be able to sell a client on it. And even if someone can't get invoices paid, they may be great at reporting and metrics.

The trick is to be competent at all of these...and I've yet to meet anyone who's truly naturally competent at *all* of it. Learning and practice are critical steps.

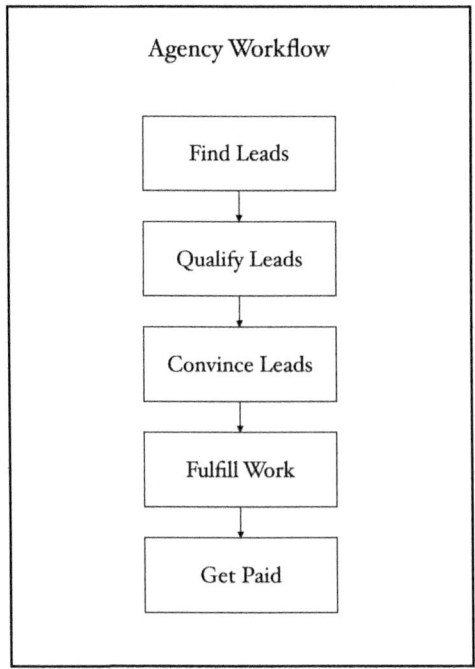

The first step on the path is finding the leads in the first place, and this is the most important, non-negotiable factor in either the short-term or long-term success of any digital agency. If you don't have potential clients, you will not have an agency. End of story.

There are many methods of finding these leads, and in our Getting Leads chapter we'll look at several of them in detail. The method that you choose will be highly dependent upon your soft skills, your technical expertise, your career history, your social cohesion, your ability to sell, and what sort of influence and authority you've been able to create within your niche. There isn't one single perfect way — but there are many possibilities.

Discosloth generates leads by creating authoritative content within our domain of expertise. There are a few reasons why this works so well for us, but I'm well aware that it won't work for everyone. Not everybody can (or even *wants* to!) spend most of their work day writing like I do. The first content that really knocked our lead ball out of the park was created in our first year: the *Beginner's Guide to PPC*, a seven-part exhaustive intro to paid search that we published on our website for free. Thanks to the generous amplification of this guide by some marketing folks (including Rand Fishkin, the author of the original *Beginner's Guide To SEO*) this piece of content went minor-league viral and reached several thousand marketers the first few days of our release. This not only kickstarted a trickle of some of our first organic client leads, but it gave us the realization that this was the channel we needed to double down on.

We followed this up by writing a full-fledged book called *Becoming A Digital Marketer*, which had a slow initial start but soon shifted to selling quite a few copies. Within a couple years of publishing this book, it was selling several hundred copies a month and was in the syllabus for a dozen or so universities around the world (to this day, one of the most surprising and fortunate projects we've worked on).

But that's not the only way. Creating content does work, but it's definitely not the only way. Some people are great at speaking publicly at conferences. That's something that Anya has done in the past, but it hasn't been something we're either very good at or very interested in pursuing. Some people are great at cold calling. I can't think of anything that frightens me more. Some people are great at networking in person. This is something that I *do* like, and we've gotten a fair share of work from our own personal contacts. Whether it's old bosses, neighbors, former coworkers, or people shacked up at the booth next to you in the coffeeshop, both Anya and I are social enough that we've been able to get some well-intentioned and natural referrals from folks that trust us.

The second step on the path is qualifying the leads you do get.

This step is something that shifts over time. At the beginning, when you're first starting out, it's pretty much unavoidable that you'll take on any work you can get. It's just what happens. You gotta do what you gotta do. However, as your revenue increases, your work load fills up, and you realize you're starting to get busy, you can also get pickier.

And when you get pickier, your clients become far, far better folks to work with. They pay more, pay faster, are more hands-off, trust you more, see better results, you name it — the up-market clients are literally always better clients.

When we first started, we were hungry for anything. We took on clients at laughably low rates. I remember one of our first ongoing clients, which was a taxi service somewhere in Europe, and we literally charged him $35 per month.

That's not a typo. Looking at it now, it's a little mind-bogglingly low. *But it's just what we had to do.* We wanted work...any work.

Often in this book I'll mention the fact that you need to charge what you're worth, and pricing higher inevitably leads to better clients. Eventually, your $35/mo clients turn into $5,000/mo clients. But at the beginning, we needed anything. And it turns out, we got that client via a small marketing agency that was trying to add PPC to their service range. To this day, we are still getting clients from them (which pay more than $35 per month!) and have made an agency friend which has been growing as well since we've been working together.

The third step is sales: convincing solid leads of the fact that you're the best choice for them. A lot of folks hate sales for a variety of reasons. Unfortunately, these same folks avoid it like the plague, and that's one of the many reasons their agencies spiral downwards into a sucking maelstrom of profitability and cashflow issues.

Sales is often inaccurately equated to high-pressure, hard-push tactics — like some sort of late-night infomercial coming at you live from a used car lot. Some folks do use these tactics in digital marketing, but high-pressure bro sales is not something that I've done or something that I've seen any reputable marketer do.

Sales is different for every agency, every client, and every vertical, but for me it looks like this: I pick up the phone when a lead calls, we chat about things like their new grandkids or our trip to Egypt, I take a look through their Google Ads account and let them know how I would re-structure the campaign if it was up to Discosloth, and then over the course of the next few casual emails we hammer out their goals, and send them our initial invoice.

Sales, for Discosloth at least, is really just the process of developing genuine relationships. We're picky about the leads that make it through our vetting process. We actually *like* the people we work with. It's not really hard to work with people you like...and neither is it hard to "sell".

The fourth step is delivery. You've gone through the hard steps...finding leads, vetting leads, selling leads...and now you actually have to fulfill your end of the bargain.

Plenty of agencies can do all of the above. They make money, short term, because they're good at accumulating and selling. But they don't tend to last very long...they're unsustainable because they can't effectively deliver on their promises. The average length of time of an agency/client relationship is reducing every year. In 1984, the average agency/client relationship lasted for 7.2 years. Right now, it's under 3 years, and that number is dropping.[4]

You have to be *good* at what you're doing. *Real* good. And if you can't be real good at everything, you need to niche down. You can do it yourself, you can hire freelancers, you can hire employees. Whichever way you do it, it needs to be done, and it can't be half-assed. We'll cover fulfillment in several different chapters, looking at where to find talent and how to communicate results. This keeps them around for next month's retainer fee.

---

[4] American Association of Advertising Agencies, *"Average Tenure of Client Agency Relationships"*

And that brings us to our final step, which is getting paid. There's a lot packed into here. Initial pricing, one-off versus ongoing payments, recurring revenue, invoicing and billing methods, the risks and benefits of various models, contracts, and endless cells in an infinite amount of spreadsheets.

I have walked through the payment & billing process of countless agencies, and without fail there is a simple way of avoiding cashflow issues.

I once wrote back to an agency owner who was bringing in some very respectable income, but he was desperate about finding the right business banking account for himself. Finding the right business bank account was a matter of life and death for his agency. He was upset at his current bank because, after accepting a payment, it took around 2-3 days before he could withdraw revenue and pay his contractors, and he couldn't keep enough cash on hand to make it work.

"This seems like a simple issue," I wrote back. "You're charging after the work is done, and this is making you late on paying your contractors. This is setting you up for massive cashflow problems in the future, the sort that torpedoes your whole business if something unforeseen happens, like if a client defaults on you, or your bank puts a temporary hold on something. It's set up for failure."

I don't think the agency owner liked that, because he charged based on a pricing model that is super difficult to scale (performance-based and ad spend percentage) but the solution was clear. "Invoice up front, and either charge everything at the beginning of the month before you start work (best case) or at the most net 15 or net 30. Pay your contractors on a monthly basis rather than one-off payments for each project."

With all of these factors in play, the path from square one to payday can appear long and complicated. It may seem daunting, but at the same time, I think it's simpler than it appears. The key is developing a mindset of slow, sustainable, patient, steady, profitable, and cash-positive growth.

It takes time; but the payoff is worth it.

Chapter Takeaways

....

1. Determine your definition of success in a quantifiable manner. Is it money? Is it time? Is it lifestyle? Is it more time with your family? Is it scale? For example, is your definition of success a *$200,000/year income?* Is it a *35-hour work week?* Is it *at least 3 employees?* Or is it *1 extra day off per week?*

2. Determine how you want to get leads. Are you good at cold calling, or do you hate the idea of talking to strangers? Are you good at writing, or are you better at creating YouTube videos? Do you have an extensive local business network? All these are factors in how you could approach lead generation.

3. Determine what sort of clients you want to work with. How will you qualify them: by their budget, location, or industry vertical?

4. Determine how you want to deliver your agency work. Are you going to deliver it yourself, or hire full-time employees, or contract freelancers?

5. Think about how you want your business model to look: fee-based, commission, hours. What stands out to you?

MAKE OR BREAK FACTORS

"Many dreams come true, and some have silver linings." — Led Zeppelin,
Over the Hills and Far Away

I think there are five make or break factors for a successful micro-agency — elements that are highly conducive to sustainability and growth. These are the factors that have helped Discosloth become what it is:

1. Specialization
2. Simplicity
3. Brand
4. Cashflow/Profit
5. Revenue Adjacency

Specialization can take many forms. With us, it evolved over the years. We didn't start as a specialized agency. That process took a few years, in which we whittled down the services we provided, and eventually landed on the single thing we did best: paid search.

Focusing on our specialty brought a lot of benefits, most of all the ability to stand out within our field. It's hard to stand out in a field when your agency is a jack of all trades...and if you don't stand out, client acquisition is going to be much harder.

Simplicity could also be worded as efficiency. Our processes and business models have always been simple, but at first it was more out of necessity. The first year, we simply couldn't afford *not* to run things simply. Then, we realized that keeping things simple was massively valuable. Needlessly complex processes, tools, policies, and lines of communication are an easy trap to fall into. I've seen agencies try to go complex far too soon, and they stop getting as much actual work done.

Brand is critical. So much so that I should probably place it at the very top of the list. Our brand allows us to have an amazing level of organic client acquisition, a level of trust already established before people even pick up the phone to call us, and in turn this gives us the ability to be far pickier about the sort of clients we work with.

Cashflow/Profit could simply be described as *bringing in more money than we spend*. And not just in the long run: this needs to happen every single month. So many agencies bring on massive amounts of debt in an attempt to scale. That's a death knell and will ensure financial problems the instant a black swan event happens (which could be anything from losing a big client to a global economy collapse).

And finally, revenue adjacency. Being close to your client's bottom line is important. The closer you can be to your client's profits, the better. And if you can prove it via attribution or data in some manner, even better. Think about it: as an agency, or a specialist, or even a freelancer, our entire jobs pivot around the ability to make more money for our clients. If we can do that, and continually prove it, there's nothing better for job security.

	Take Your Pick	
Specialization (in technical niche or industry served)	———————	Non-specialized (jack-of-all-trades)
Operate Simply & Efficiently	———————	Complex Operations & Overhead
Likable, Memorable Brand	———————	Forgettable or Unlikable Brand
Positive Cashflow & High Margins	———————	Negative Cashflow & Low Margins
Important to Client's Revenue	———————	Unimportant to Client's Revenue

Keep these five elements in mind as we go further and discuss in more detail. Essentially, these tangible elements serve as a way to explain the abstract factors of a successful agency.

Of course there is more than one way to build a great agency, but you wouldn't want the opposite. Nobody wants to build an un-specialized, complex, poorly branded, cash-bleeding agency who can't tie their results to any benefit for the client.

On the other hand, a specialized, simple, well-branded, prof-itable agency which attributes revenue-based results with data? This is positioned for success.

Chapter Takeaways

....

1. Which specialization stands out to you: technical specialization (for example, specializing in ecommerce analytics) or industry/vertical specialization (for example, specializing in the construction industry)?

2. How can you keep your agency as minimal and straightforward as possible, with no extraneous and complicating aspects? What sorts of work and processes do you want to avoid?

3. Having a solid, communicable brand is critical. What sort of a brand do you want your agency to portray?

4. Do you have the savings to start up an agency without taking on significant debt? Do you think it is possible to always have positive cashflow, every month?

5. How will your agency be revenue-adjacent (AKA, how can you communicate your results to your clients in terms of ROI)?

FINDING YOUR AGENCY'S NICHE

"The most valuable businesses of coming decades will be built by entrepre-neurs who seek to empower people rather than try to make them obsolete." -
Peter Thiel[5]

At the beginning of this book I mentioned that if you are set-ting out to create the world's next Dentsu, Omnicom, or Publicis, you need to shut this book immediately.

That expectation is perhaps a little absurd, but you'll have to forgive me for my hyperbole. What's not absurd, however, is the fact that the majority of potential agency founders start the process wanting to start a full-service agency.

This isn't an unreasonable approach. When we started our agency, it was exactly what we planned on doing: creating a digital agency doing everything we knew how to do.

Most skilled digital marketers today will have a large array of talents at their fingertips. There is no shortage of marketers with

---

[5] Peter Thiel, *Zero To One: Notes on Startups, or How to Build the Future* (2014)

great technical skills. The instinct, when starting an agency, is to put them all to good use.

The problem with this strategy is that everyone else knows how to do what you're doing, too — and there is no way you can set yourself apart from the crowd.

You may be the absolute best in the world at one thing (conversion rate optimization, for example) but there is no way on earth that you are the best in the world at conversion rate optimization, Google Shopping campaigns, automating email funnels, *and* e-commerce website design.

All of this serves to illustrate the point that a new agency can't do everything. And it can't serve everyone, either. You are now competing in a global world where a web developer from Ukraine can compete with an email marketer from Chandigarh and a copywriter from Phoenix. There are millions of people out there, and it's only getting more crowded as we speak.

There is still a lot of room for competition within two specific avenues.

The first is the technical avenue, based solely upon hard skills. Niching down into a technical skill is fantastic, especially if you truly are exceptional at this particular skill. And you're not limited by volume, either. The more specific you are, the better. There are entire million-dollar agencies built around setting up Shopify analytics dashboards for fledgling e-commerce retailers. There are entire boutique shops built around setting up email drop campaigns for local contractors. There are wildly successful companies that only do SEO for WooCommerce.

The second is the industry avenue...choosing a vertical based upon the intended client. Getting into this avenue is usually dependent upon your past career and experience, but it makes for great word-of-mouth, instant referrals, and usually it's quite easy to acclimate to the vertical's idiosyncrasies of jargon, profit margins, and status quo.

Niching down has its downsides. One of those is the lack of diversification. You may have the fear that the need for your specific technical skill may go away, or you may be at risk of your entire industry vertical folding up.

And it's a very real risk, but at the end of the day I'm not sure it's much riskier than starting a full-service, jack-of-all-trades ad agency which never goes anywhere. Paying careful attention to the current tech landscape and staying on top of technical advancements can help you foresee the need for a potential pivot years in advance.

The industry avenue could be trickier, since all your eggs can be in one vertical's basket, but this highly depends upon the avenue. I know of one guy who operated an ad agency serving travel & hospitality clients. He was knocking it out of the park, until spring 2020 happened — and governments closed borders everywhere, forcing hotels & airlines to shut down. His company lost the majority of revenue immediately.

At Discosloth, we chose to pursue niching down into a technical skill. We are industry agnostic, since we view having a wide range of clients as a form of diversification. It's definitely still a risk that PPC advertising disappears altogether one day, but it's been around for 20 years and we think it'll be around, in some form or the other, for another 20 years.

Becoming a specialist brings along both downsides and benefits. Specializing means that you can charge more, you will pick up a lot more referral clients, you will be more readily recognized as an authority in your niche, and you can easily scale since your process will be simple and you won't spend a lot of time testing and experimenting. Unfortunately, it also ties you to the ebb and flow of success within that particular specialization, so you're a little dependent upon factors outside of your control. In almost all cases, I have seen specialist agencies *start slower* but *end up stronger*. This is because it can take a lot of time and patience to get into a specific niche, but once you're in it, the going is far, far easier.

Starting an agency which is a "jack-of-all-trades, do-it-all" agency providing a little bit of everything is far easier to do right off the bat. These agencies almost always *start faster* but *end up weaker*. If they do well, it's usually because they end up pivoting to either a service-specific agency or a full-service agency which serves clients in only one very specific industry. Full-service agencies have one major downside: they are always having to chase down clients and do a lot of outbound sales, even years down the road. Full-service agencies tend to require hiring full-time account executives to keep adding new business. Niche agencies tend to accumulate inbound leads and referrals over the years, something that's far harder for the full-service agency to do. For full-service agencies, it's easier at the beginning because there is no shortage of general work: website design, graphic design, branding, PPC, analytics, SEO, you name it.

This makes it easier for the full-service agency to reach "ramen profitability" sooner, but it also makes it harder to break out of the rat race and start truly scaling in both volume and profit. The problem with full-service agencies? There is nothing innate that sets them apart from any other full-service agency, and without a specialty, referrals and brand recognition are far less likely.

It's also worth noting that by saying your agency doesn't need to be full-service, this does *not* mean you shouldn't have any knowledge about other specializations. For example, a PPC expert who doesn't know the basics of SEO isn't a very good PPC expert, because that expert won't know how to analyze the client's SEO data to make their paid campaigns perform better. Or, an analytics expert who doesn't know basic web development (at least how to navigate the backend of a website) is likely not going to be the best analytics expert since they won't be able to easily find the root cause of any tracking issues. You don't necessarily need to be the best at everything, but you *do* need to understand the basics of everything.

As I'll mention later on, during the first couple years of Discosloth's existence, we tried to sell a broad range of services before we realized that wasn't the best strategy for us. But, the benefit of doing this was that we learned a lot about each service. Even now, if a client is experiencing some sort of problem outside our direct purview, we have enough breadth of experience in various aspects of digital marketing that we can easily point them in the right direction and explain how all of the channels are working together.

My advice is to learn and understand it all, but *choose one skill to master.*

WHAT SERVICES SHOULD YOUR AGENCY OFFER?

So how do you find your new agency's service offer?

As the founder, this decision likely rests upon your own strengths and weaknesses. Without a doubt, you will have a few technical strengths to rely upon. And without a doubt, you will have career experience in certain industries more than others. Whether those technical strengths and industry experiences are actually lucrative is another matter entirely.

When I read marketing articles online, especially oriented to career development or anything involving running an agency, I find that authors have a tendency to approach the profitability of niches — whether we're talking about technical niches or industry verticals — with a sort of agnosticism. It's almost like nobody wants to take sides and offend folks in a certain niche, which I understand. And it's definitely possible to make a lot of money in a lot of niches, so there are outliers everywhere.

But we're not here to assuage a social media manager's financial ego, are we? It's worth knowing which niches are truly lucrative, and which are over-populated, and which are fading away. Keep in mind that, as I mentioned above, there are outliers everywhere. But medians don't lie, and it's worth laying out the losers and the gainers for everyone to see.

The reality is that some technical niches are profitable, and others are going the way of the dodo bird. It's important to be realistic about this.

We will look at the following technical verticals that are commonly served by digital agencies:

1. Social media marketing (SMM)

2. Search engine optimization (SEO)

3. Pay-per-click advertising (PPC)

4. Web design

5. Branding

6. Graphic design

7. Copywriting

8. Email marketing

10. Conversion rate optimization (CRO)

11. Web Analytics

12. PR/Influencer marketing

The first, social media marketing, can be divided into two categories: paid social and organic social.

A purely organic social manager focuses on maintaining the online presence of a brand across platforms, updating statuses and adding content and increasing engagement, all without using paid ads. This is the position most people think about when they think about social media management. It's also the niche that was all the rage in my senior year of college, was the entry level position which most of my peers went into, and was the position that they left as soon as possible so that they could afford to pay rent (this includes myself). I do not see social media management as the best niche for an agency to attempt. To be clear, there *are* agencies who are succeeding at this. To be successful on social media, you need to make sure you are good at storytelling, growing audiences, and being relatable to those same audiences. The main issue? Most people think this is easier than it actually is. If you think that you can just post a picture with some text every Monday, Wednesday, and Friday at 4pm, your new agency is doomed for failure. It requires storytelling, branding, expertise, and a little bit of daring. If you want to see a perfect example of social media done well, check out something like the Wendy's Twitter account.

Paid social, which involves ad platforms, is where you can actually make a bit of money. Due to the complexity and frustration of working with social media ad platforms, you can make a decent chunk of change by becoming a master at these platforms. The downsides, in my eyes, include a dependency upon the platforms for success, and a fairly hectic world in which tactics and costs change constantly. But keeping up to date in this is part of the "barrier to entry" that gives paid social agencies a benefit in charging a premium. Paid social is about making sure you understand the audience of your client, and it is a little more complex than merely guessing who you want to target. Analytics is a critical skill for paid social. You don't want to just guess who your client's audience is based upon either your or your client's bias. Just because you're trying to sell colognes to men does *not* mean men are the ones buying them the most. It may be girlfriends, for example, and the only way you can know that is through analytics. Pairing paid social with analytics skills may be your way of succeeding.

The second, SEO, is one of the most polarizing and difficult to quantify of them all. It's an industry in which I myself have extensive experience — and one which I ultimately ended up leaving. The biggest problem with SEO as a niche is that the charlatans and gurus outnumber the real experts by 100 to 1. This drags down the credibility of the niche massively, and along with this you'll also experience higher expectations, lower fees, and more overall stress. SEO is still alive and will be for a very long time: the problem is that there are a hundred million other people out there who *also* think they are expert SEOs. It's one of those industries where, if you have made it, you've *made* it. If you haven't, it's going to be one of the most difficult things you've ever done. You will either make a million dollars a year, or barely pay rent. There is little room for moderation in the wild west of SEO. This world has changed so much, over time. It started in the late 90s through the late 2010s by being good at tricking the system (you could see results simply by copy/pasting lists of keywords into the page and turning the text white!) Now, it is more about quality content and branding paired with solid web development and optimization.

Pay-per-click advertising (PPC) holds a special place in my heart since it is the channel that Discosloth has focused on and thrived in. It is an extremely difficult niche in which to become a true expert — but this difficulty serves as a massive barrier to entry. And that's a good thing when it comes to competition. It's perhaps the most technical of all digital marketing disciplines except for analytics, but it requires so much expertise in analytics as well, that it serves as an additional barrier to entry. If you're technically inclined I couldn't recommend any niche more than this one...if you're *not* technically inclined, I couldn't *discourage* it more. Since a PPC specialist is so intimately connected with a business balance sheet, you can charge accordingly. I personally believe it is the most lucrative (if also least sexy and most boring) of all digital marketing disciplines. I see this as a perfect niche for folks that neither feel like they're super creative — nor want to do something really boring in business intelligence or finance. It's also great for people who want to see results fast, and be able to make changes *now*. Especially in paid search (Google Ads, Microsoft Ads, Amazon Ads) you can gather more granular data than perhaps any other marketing niche.

Web design has changed so much over the years. I remember the first website I built sometime in 2003, teaching myself HTML by looking at the code my copy of Macromedia Dreamweaver generated. This was before WordPress even existed, and back when being a webmaster was a lucrative and exclusive position. Throughout my high school years, while my peers had summer jobs serving cherry limeades at Sonic or mowing lawns or sitting at reception desks, I built websites. I did this throughout college and even well into my twenties. I did this for years, until eventually I came to the realization that the field had outstripped me. Now, web design has evolved into a highly polarized field: it is either point-and-click, or it is months-long intensive development. You can either generate a site within any number of web platforms like WordPress or Webflow, or plan out a deeply involved custom development process of Docker and Python and Redis and MySQL. You simply can't charge much for a simple templated WordPress site any more...perhaps a few thousand bucks if you're lucky. But if you have a full development team, you can charge a few *hundred thousand bucks* for a custom site. This field has become both impoverished and filled with riches. The earnings limit is technical skill.

I'm including branding and graphic design in the same group, not because they are the same as each other, but because their economics essentially are the same. When it comes to marketing and dollars, it is no secret that technical skills are rewarded more highly than creative skills. I'm not saying that's nice to hear, but it's the truth. I have never seen a creative agency which makes as much consistent take-home revenue, at the end of the year, as a technical agency. It simply does not exist. There are few companies in the world which will pay for creative. We can't all get the Apple or Nike account, unfortunately. This is one of those unique fields in which a *freelancer* creative can make far more money than a creative *agency*. There is no shortage of creatives making solid incomes. There is, however, a massive shortage of creative agencies who actually pay the bills.

Copywriting, however, is one of the creative fields which can be well rewarded, even if a freelance gig scales into an agency. The problem is, good copywriting is very hard to find, and people almost always overestimate their copywriting skills. It's such a subjective ability — one in which you really only know it when you see it, but it's hard to describe otherwise — that the only way to become successful in copywriting is to develop your personal brand by sheer dedication, time, and generation of excellent content.

Email marketing is a hidden gem. It sounds like the sort of thing only a very old guy would get into. It sounds boring. It sounds out of date. And just because of that, it is one of the most lucrative and under-served niches in all of digital marketing. The analytics and platforms involved in a well-structured email marketing campaign are actually so much more complex than you'd think, that the technical abilities required are huge barriers to entry...especially since you have to pair it with copywriting. Email marketing is a massively profitable channel for many companies (often the ROI outstrips any other channel) which means that you can charge lucrative fees in return for your expertise. I have always secretly wanted to start an email agency, but it's so far out of my orbit that it will have to wait for someone else.

Conversion rate optimization, or CRO, is often paired with user experience, or UX. I've seen quite a few CRO/UX agencies start over the years, and do well. It's a heavily analytics-dependent niche which also requires integration with other marketing channels and a decent amount of web development. Analyzing, optimizing, and developing strategy for website performance can be a huge boon to companies that are looking to scale and improve, so they will pay for CRO. The industry, however, has its share of incompetence as gurus around the world try to dip their toes in the field. It's a very interesting niche in which to start an agency, as long as you have extensive experience and proven results in CRO.

Analytics is something that we work in extensively, mostly offered in tandem with our paid search work. It is critical for the success of any other marketing channel, and even more critical for e-commerce. It's a highly technical field that doesn't interest most marketers, so it's something that is great to master as it sets you apart. To be successful as an agency specifically offering analytics services, you can't just be a "Google Analytics person". You'll need to be an agency which works closely with databases, CRMs, business intelligence tools like Power BI or Tableau, constantly analyzing information and patterns to help your client's business grow. It's probably the service which furthest from traditional marketing as possible, but still one of the most important ones as far as enabling other marketing efforts to see maximum results.

Digital PR, or what is starting to be called "influencer marketing" is what many aspects of traditional SEO is heading towards. While SEO, properly speaking, is highly technical, many parts of traditional search engine optimization (like link building) are becoming more of a journalistic pursuit. Digital PR is not easy, and as it's evolving so quickly, it's my assumption that those who choose to pursue this career will need to start in some other form of marketing first. Experience is critical in this niche, and it's not something you can easily "churn out" without knowing your industry like the back of your hand.

CHOOSING A NICHE WITH RECURRING REVENUE

Outside of the skillset considerations of starting an agency in a certain technical niche, I think the most important element of developing a sustainable, profitable agency is cashflow.

Without predictable, scalable, and steady cashflow, you're going to have a hard time taking your agency from year one to year five...or client 1 to client 25.

I encourage folks to start agencies in fields that facilitate ongoing income with long-term clients. Some technical niches are more conducive to this than others. Other technical niches are very difficult to create ongoing, almost passive-style income from.

Good examples of niches that are conducive to ongoing income are service and management-focused, like PPC, email marketing, SEO, public relations, social media management, since these are places where you can expect monthly recurring work to happen.

Niches in which it is much harder to create recurring revenue are project-focused, like web design, branding, logo design, or analytics. It's worth noting that it's not impossible; it's just not conducive. It is very possible to create add-on services or long-term contracts within these niches. But, generally, a web design agency will make the most money when they land a single one-off big contract...not by their sources of recurring revenue, which are usually things like reselling hosting or offering maintenance contracts. A branding company nearly always gets a brand redesign project *one* time (hopefully, if they're doing their job right, the client won't come back next year for another redesign!) Similarly, a web design company who lands a major site redesign project hopefully does their job well enough that they don't have to do *another* site redesign the following year. Analytics agencies have a bit more flexibility since they can not only implement analytics, but also offer ongoing services to interpret and present business intelligence...but they're still going to make the most money on one-time implementation projects.

It's worth remembering that I'm not disparaging these sorts of agencies *at all*. I'm just pointing out that they don't necessarily line up well with our specific approach of building a super-profitable and super-sustainable micro-agency. As co-founders of a micro-agency that focuses on consistent, predictable cashflow, we have a clear preference for recurring revenue, and those are best offered in niches other than web design or branding.

PPC campaigns, SEO work, email strategies, social management, none of these are one-off niches. They all require constant ongoing work. You can't just start up a PPC campaign and let it run for eternity, at least if you want to maximize your return on investment. It needs weekly if not daily babying.

That's where the most important factor of choosing a service niche comes in: cashflow. Find a niche that requires a little bit of work spread out over a long time, rather than a niche that requires a lot of work crammed into a short time.

It's slow but consistent growth, rather than feast or famine.

You don't have to find new clients all the time. The same clients will come back to you. They need more of the same.

With predictable recurring revenue, burnout, stress, deadlines, deliverables, and exhaustion won't be as much of a factor. Cashflow, profit margin, predictability, and ultimately scalability will be better. And, in the end, I think you'll have a healthier agency that gives you more take-home revenue at the end of each and every month.

A final bit of advice that we suggest is this: when you start your agency, make sure *you* have the right skillsets for it. If you don't have any any interest or skills in PPC, don't start a pay-per-click agency just because you think it's easier to make money. In the micro-agency fulfillment model — which we'll cover later on in other chapters — you really won't be able to rely on contractors to provide the level of service you need. After all, how can you tell that your contractor even *has* the skillset if you don't even have it?

We've seen this pattern play out more than once in agencies: owners who outsource everything rarely have the skillset to know what's going on, so they promise results to clients that are impossible to realistically achieve. Then, both the agency and the contractor fails because of the initial expectations and promises which were made.

Start with something you know.

If you're an amazing copywriter, find a way to be the best at that, and identify the ideal customer niche to be profitable within. This way, you'll be able to retain more profit in the beginning, when you really need cashflow as you're starting out. As time goes on, you'll be able to hire additional people to do the work for you.

When Anya and I started Discosloth, we used our own personal skillsets. Anya excels at web analytics and PPC, while I excel at creative aspects like branding and writing. If you feel like you're lacking in specific skills, that may be an indication that getting a cofounder is a good idea.

Chapter Takeaways

....

1. Determine which technical niche you'd like to work in. What are the benefits and downsides of this niche? (Every niche has both!)

2. Agencies which have a solid recurring revenue base tend to be more financially sustainable than agencies which only have one-off projects. How would your agency develop recurring revenue?

3. Niching down makes starting & running a micro-agency easier, but it also comes with risk. How would you mitigate the risks that come with choosing one particular industry or service?

4. What are *you* good at?

5. Do you feel that you need to find a co-founder?

BUILDING YOUR AGENCY'S BRAND

"Gosh, you've really got some nice toys here." – Blade Runner (1982)

If there is a single thing that most agencies should have done from the beginning, it's that they should have cultivated a strong agency brand.

Branding is one of those criminally underrated aspects of marketing that is almost impossible to objectively quantify, but it pays off in the long run. Ironically, branding specialists haven't done a great job of branding themselves, so they'll rarely get paid as much as they could for branding someone else's new enterprise.

An agency's brand is not merely its name, logo, color palette, typography, and overall look & feel, although those factors are all critical elements. It's also the agency's *personality*, and in most cases this personality needs to be an extension of the founder's personality.

Let's hope that *your* personality is on point, then, right? I think that's just a given, since you are going to be the primary pivot of the entire business. You're going to be the first point of all sales, the first point of all customer service, and the first point of production and delivery as well, at least for the first year or two. Either you or your cofounder *has* to be able to express who they are to the world...otherwise your agency is going to be lost in a sea of better-branded competitors.

I'd like to use our own agency as a case study for branding, because I think it's something we do exceptionally well. If we were to be prodded, I think both Anya and I would admit that branding (both personal and company-specific) was a primary factor in our success.

HOW WE DEVELOPED OUR OWN BRAND

Our agency's name is Discosloth. Our mascot is a neon pink-and-blue sloth. Our wordmark is a hot pink heavy metal font.

On the surface, it's the most unprofessional, bold, and non-serious brand that an agency could possibly have short of something scribbled out with crayons and Comic Sans.

Yet, that hasn't stopped Discosloth from having a client roster with some Fortune 500 companies, getting press in *The New York Times* and *The Washington Post*, and managing multi-million dollar Google Ads accounts.

None of this was accidental or unintentional (fortunate, to be sure) but this was our strategy from day one. Both Anya and I, before we cofounded Discosloth, came from a corporate startup background in which we felt both creatively and strategically suppressed. We couldn't test things without limitations, we couldn't deploy stuff without approvals, and we couldn't design anything unless by com-

Our website looks like this. Who would trust a sloth to do reports?

mittee.

When we left our jobs and started Discosloth, therefore, we knew we were going to do it the way we wanted. We also knew what we *didn't* want.

We didn't want corporate jargon, with clients focused on assigning arbitrary quarterly KPIs and making us fill out customer persona analyses. We didn't want daily meetings, agile sprints, complex contracts, or 90-day payment terms. We didn't want to bid on RFPs. We didn't want to become a traditional ad agency.

We wanted to make a lot of money working with clients we liked, and the ability to be our unfiltered and opinionated selves. We wanted to do *whatever we want.*

We wanted a brand that would pre-filter out the people who wouldn't jive with our vibe. We wanted our brand to attract employees that thought Discosloth was a cool name. If our brand was overly bizarre or offensive to someone's professional sensibilities — great! Let's save both of us some time.

Our first strategy meeting (which may have consisted of an entire bottle of wine) consisted primarily of finding the perfect name. Anya liked cute animals, and I liked eighties retro vibes, so we made a shortlist of ridiculous-sounding names and kept typing them into a domain search until we found one that wasn't taken. Turns out, if you take words like mega, disco, turbo, and combine them with turtle, raccoon, sloth, llama, and aardvark, you end up with Discosloth.

Our unorthodox brand has enabled us to make some unorthodox decisions. We've established unusual internal policies (like no required work hours, or paid vacation, or a yearly "13th salary" bonus, or company retreats to Egypt) and generated enough branded content to fill four books, literally.

Unintentionally, this company brand has bled over into personal brands. It's purely accidental, but once you can become transparent and expressive in one aspect (like your company brand) it starts extending further. I've gotten calls from potential leads who say things like "oh, you're the Google Ads guy with the big beard" or "you're a big Mercedes guy, right?" or "how many countries are you at, now?"

Your brand will not be the same as ours. Hopefully, it won't be the same as anyone else's, either.

While you probably don't want an agency named after a neon jungle animal, there will be a brand that fits who you are (and your cofounder, if they exist).

Some of your brand can only be determined if you know some other aspects of your future agency, like what sort of clients you will service and what sort of verticals you want to work in.

What I can wholeheartedly recommend, however, is to avoid boring names. I've worked with agency owners who strive too hard to find something deep or meaningful, but instead this ends up coming across as forced or boring. It's easy to come up with a name that's a little too on the nose, so to speak, like Signpost Advertising or Digital Advertising Experts. Nobody will remember that or even be remotely interested in the brand. If your last name is unique, that's an entirely fine approach... Katzenbalger is memorable. If your last name is Wilson, perhaps not.

Most importantly, however, is not necessarily your name or your logo or how nice of a website you run, but what sort of content and authority you push out into the world.

The means with which you push that content out there is up to you: and even the actual meat of that content is up to you, as well. You may be a great public speaker, or you may make great videos, or you could be an excellent writer. You may be great at technical education, or great at inspirational pep talks, or great at connecting with a certain demographic. But putting yourself (and your ideas) out there for others to consume is a critical part of developing your company's brand.

It can feel daunting, especially if your newfound company has a total of 4 followers on Twitter (your spouse, your brother, your mom, and some bot account from Peru) but it's just simply a waiting game. Wherever you choose to publish and amplify your content, you just have to keep on doing it. For years, if necessary.

We made the mistake, initially, of trying to be everywhere at once. Pretty soon, though, we realized that we weren't being very efficient that way.

We also realized early on that nobody wants to consume content from a company. They want to consume content from a real, live person. It makes sense. You can't really consume content generated by a company without feeling like somewhere, somehow, you're going to be sold a product.

It's easier to trust a real human face, and that's why we shifted to building our personal brand *in tandem* with our company's brand, and tying them together (perhaps inevitably and inseparably, but that's another issue altogether).

Becoming the authority means being someone whom people trust. It means giving away a lot of valuable information. It means being generous with your time and knowledge, even if there is no direct monetary reward. It may seem exhausting in the meantime, but it pays off handsomely.

We released our first "company" content in early 2018. It wasn't just a blog post. It was an in-depth, multi-chapter, detailed micro-site which we also compiled as a detailed PDF. It took us months upon months to write.

We decided to release it for absolutely free. It could have easily been packaged and sold as a Udemy course (and we considered that) but we realized that in the early stages of our company, reach and amplification may be far more important than any income we receive from a course. This turns out to have been one of the best decisions we could have made. Because it was free, it got recommended even more by people. We started getting upwards of two thousand visitors a day to our new *Beginner's Guide To PPC*, especially after the author of the original *Beginner's Guide To SEO*, Rand Fishkin of Moz fame, shared the link to his hundreds of thousands of followers.

It's worth a short detour to share that story. Rand Fishkin didn't share our guide out of nowhere. I had been engaging on his posts on Twitter for some time, especially back when I was more involved in SEO. He released an amazing tool on his website (a link aggregator that compiled all the most popular marketing-related news articles). I emailed him thanking him for the usefulness of the new tool. I mentioned that we'd created a new PPC guide partially inspired by the usefulness of his famous SEO guide, and that we'd love for him to offer critique on ours before we released it into the wild.

Entirely unexpectedly, Rand responded and offered to amplify the *Beginner's Guide To PPC.*

Rand Fishkin <rand@sparktor...   Tue, May 29, 2018, 3:48 PM   ☆   ↩   ⋮
to Gil ▾

Hi Gil - I think this is really well done! I found it readable, accessible, easy to get
through, and thoughtfully composed. Bravo. So many people have sent me guides
like this over the years and this is honestly one of the few I found compelling.
Congrats!

Are you amplifying it yet? Happy to help when you're ready to launch

He did so, and we were blown away.

I didn't ask him to share it; I just wanted honest feedback.

Turns out, free and valuable content works. Very few folks will recommend a paid resource unless it's *the* industry standard. There are thousands of paid course creators out there, all competing to sell their expertise. It *can* work, to be sure, but even better is spending the same amount of time and then giving away something for free.

We followed up this free guide's publication with more content...a full entry-level intro to digital marketing book called *Becoming A Digital Marketer,* a book-formatted edition of the *Beginner's Guide To PPC,* and then a business-oriented book on remote work which was an admitted total flop.

This established Discosloth as a brand...and has resulted in a steady stream of inbound client inquiries for years now.

To this day, we are still seeing results from the work we did in our first few years. As of 2022, the *Beginner's Guide to PPC* is being translated into book format by one of France's largest publishing houses, in partnership with one of the most progressive Paris digital ad agencies. We likely won't get a single client directly from that (we don't even speak French, after all!) but the branding is invaluable.

We wanted a brand that was open. We wanted to be very transparent about who runs Discosloth, and what our processes and strategies are. We wanted a brand that was generous, giving away everything we create for free whenever possible. We wanted a brand that implied we weren't just an average safe pick when it comes to finding a PPC partner. This attracts the sort of clientele that we like to talk with...people who are intrigued by who we are as people.

The danger with using just any other company as a case study is that it can seem easy, or foolproof.

Building Discosloth was neither easy nor foolproof.

We made mistake after mistake while starting Discosloth, and to be honest we did not have our entire business model planned out when we started. If we had, we'd have been able to focus earlier on and start generating the right sort of content more effectively.

The biggest brand misstep was at the beginning: assuming we'd be a full-service digital agency. We thought we would be able to do content marketing, analytics, paid search, search engine optimization, web design, and email marketing. Not only was this an error in terms of business model, it was an error in terms of brand.

It was a dilution of what we did best, and while I'm glad we eventually found out what we needed to focus on, it did take us a couple years before we gained the courage to say *no* to everything extraneous.

The last time we didn't say no, it was for an existing PPC client who drastically needed help redoing their marketing site. Even though we knew we didn't need to get distracted by the project, we did it anyway. I charged around $12,000 (not a small amount for us at the time) but within days we knew it was a mistake, and I swore we would never get distracted again.

It's hard to say *no* to $12,000 but it ended up costing us. By sucking my attention away from our important ongoing PPC clients, quality waned on all fronts, the project dragged on far longer than it needed to, and by the time it was finished I had *had* it. Sending that final email with the final deliverables off into the ether was like an invisible weight had been lifted off our shoulders.

What Should Your Website Be Like?

Notice that it's not a question. You *must* have a website. Even though you may not use it extensively, and publishing lots of material on it is entirely optional, your clients *will* research you and your brand, and they will click on the first thing that appears.

Having a clean, professional website is critical. No buts or ifs about it. A short, memorable domain name is important. Nothing is worse than researching a marketing freelancer, consultant, or agency, and then discovering their website is a hot mess of default templates, poor fonts, janky code, and questionable design choices. Even worse is trying to find out anything about them, as people, and not finding anything on the site at all.

A small agency thrives on trust. If you don't know where, what, or who is behind a random domain name online, how are you going to develop any level of trust?

Think about it in terms of a client. They're looking for help with their online marketing. They're wanting to pay a professional

$2000 per month to help with their ad campaigns. They have narrowed it down to two options.

One of their options has real photos and names of the staff members. They have an about page detailing their experience and history. They've spoken at a handful of local events, and they've got a few blog posts about industry insights.

The other option simply lists their services on the website. There are not any photos of the team, there are no names, there isn't a location indicated. For all you know, this could be a 50-person company located in Toronto, or it could be a single guy located in Indonesia. You never know.

Which will they pick?

Sometimes a client wants to hire a single dude behind a laptop screen. Sometimes a client wants to hire the 50-person company. Either way, if you don't tell them, they'll be disappointed.

It is always better to be honest, even if you are a two-person micro-agency. Trying to be bigger than you are never works, is always obvious, and can actually harm you.

Just be honest, straightforward, and very transparent. There isn't anything to be ashamed of. There's no reason for hiding your real name from your clients. I'm still not sure why so many fly-by-night marketers do so. It's entirely within your right to operate anonymously. Just be forewarned that you're handicapping your future growth by doing so. It's hard for clients to recommend and refer a dude they only know by the name of @Jako3000.

BE WHO YOU ARE

In an industry that is crammed chock-full of newly established fly-by-night agencies, the sort that churn through clients and then fold after a couple years, authenticity is extremely rare.

Your agency — even if you're starting one in a particularly narrow niche — is still competing with hundreds or thousands of others. That's why I think it's especially important to just be who you are.

If you are a solo practitioner, don't portray yourself as an agency. You're not. Don't you think your clients will figure that out, sooner than later? If you are located in Turkey, don't try to portray yourself as an agency with an office on Madison Avenue. Your clients will pick up on that pretty quickly. And if you don't have any experience whatsoever in X service or Y vertical, don't pretend that you do. Are you presenting yourself as the CEO of a full-service agency? Well, you better have a board of directors, a receptionist, and an office as well, otherwise you're just going to look like an idiot when a client calls the 1-800 number and the CEO picks up his cell phone.

The truth always comes out, and that's why you stick with what you are. *It's entirely fine to be a three-person agency who is very good at one single thing.*

The same premise also applies to your communication, your messaging, your brand, and how you treat your customers. Don't fake it. Do what you want, and do what you're good at, and say what you mean. The authenticity, honesty, and straightforwardness is not a mark of weakness. It is a mark of integrity and professionalism.

I've run across many a professional marketer who can't say no to anything...and can't admit they don't know anything about a certain platform or channel. This inability to admit limitations isn't a selling factor for these guys...it's actually a massive drawback, they just don't realize it.

I'll be the first to admit, it's hard enough knowing everything about *one* vertical. The folks who say they know everything about every vertical are delusional at best, and dishonest at worst.

At one point a few years ago, a young marketer reached out to us after seeing some of our PPC-related content online. He was pretty desperate, but he was friendly and motivated. He'd found himself in quite an accidental predicament. He'd built himself a website (it looked great!) and created a full-service agency brand (which looked even better!) and was great at sales. He almost accidentally landed a massive client in his proven niche, which was landing page design. This client was happy with his landing pages, and then wanted him to take over their Google Ads account, which spent hundreds of thousands per year and drove most of their revenue. The problem? He was just a landing page designer, and didn't actually own an agency. He knew nothing about Google Ads.

This put him in a pickle. He couldn't farm out the work to a cheap outsourced service...this was a critical channel for the client. But he had no idea how this sort of work was priced or managed, either. He'd already promised weekly meetings, weekly reports, and a cost range to the client. I gave him a quick rundown of how much it would cost him to white-label this level of support. It simply wasn't possible due to the amount of support he'd promised. Unfortunately, he also took on even *more* work from this client, and ended up spreading himself so thin that he lost the client completely.

There are myriad reasons that an agency can lose clients, but misrepresentation is chief of them all. You simply can't promise the world and then deliver a patch of desert sand.

Chapter Takeaways

1. What specific qualities does your agency team possess that can be communicated via your brand?
2. Determine how you can communicate authority — while still being honest about your team's small size.
3. What are some of the possible downsides of pretending to be an agency that you're not? What would your limits of transparency be?

STARTING YOUR COMPANY

"Amateurs sit and wait for inspiration, the rest of us just get up and go to work." - Stephen King [6]

When you start your company, you'll either have a lot of start-up capital at your disposal, a little bit of startup capital at your disposal, or *no* startup capital at your disposal.

If you've got a lot of startup capital ready to be spent, you're in a great position — and you should utilize it! However, it's important to consider the strings which are attached to this capital. If it's your own money, fantastic. It's great to do whatever you want with your own money. If it's external money, however, this can cause some problems with the model we used to start our agency: for example, if you need to pay back a bank loan, or shuttle some of your profits to an angel investor.

Here's the thing about external funding, when it comes to starting up a digital agency. You don't really need it. Sure, having some free money on hand would make it exponentially easier for

---

[6] Stephen King, *On Writing: A Memoir of the Craft* (2000)

your first year or so. But after that, it would be more difficult to reach the same level of profitability. Your take-home is reduced (permanently, in the case of investors, and for many years in the case of a loan).

We started Discosloth by bootstrapping it, putting our own savings into it. Both Anya and I had decent jobs when we started Discosloth, but we were far from doing well. We didn't have much to spare. The good news for us? It cost *maybe* a hundred bucks to start our agency. The most expensive part was registering an LLC. The second most expensive part was the domain name, a full $12. Everything else was a mixture of our own skills: my experience in web design and branding to create our site and branding, Anya's experience in accounting and process to set up our books and organization, and both of our experience in marketing as a whole to structure our general direction. All of these may be extra expenses for folks who don't have these sorts of skills already.

If you had asked us, at any point during our first year, if we wanted investors to help us out, we would have said yes. I'm glad we didn't have that opportunity, because I'm convinced it would have been a short term gain for long term loss. Not only would it have negatively affected our take-home profits, but it would have negatively influenced our growth strategies.

There's something about hunger. It makes you really work your butt off in order to see success. If you know a paycheck is coming your way, there isn't a whole lot of motivation to go even further.

Some companies *need* startup capital. But those companies are the type that actually need to spend money in the first place — it's hard to build a factory, or a gas station, or an airport without some external funding. But a modern digital service company? As long as you have a laptop, you're good to go.

That doesn't mean you can just jump into it without any other considerations. Our model of starting an agency only works if your personal finances are in order. Even if we didn't have a lot, we had worked hard to make sure we didn't have any personal debt: this meant our living expenses were quite low. This meant that we could survive without pulling a large paycheck, even if our emergency fund wasn't quite what we would have liked.

We started our agency while we were still employed full-time. You can do the same, and that's how we were able to do it without more of an emergency fund. It was an exhausting few months of overlap, where we worked for more hours than I care to remember, but it's entirely doable. It's definitely better than the alternative, which would be sacrificing equity or assuming a debt load.

The legal aspects of starting a company will vary according to your location in the world, but in most cases it will be far easier than you suspect.

In the US, you technically won't need to do anything to start working, as we have the right to engage business as an unincorporated sole proprietor. There are advantages to formalizing your structure, however. You shouldn't let the legal process inhibit you from starting work already...but neither should you avoid formalizing any longer than necessary.

The best part about formalizing your structure (most easily as a single-member LLC) is that it's cheap, easy, and provides you with some great tax benefits. In our state, it costs $150 a year, and takes about 15 minutes to do online at the secretary of state's website.

The other great thing about running your service business under an LLC (as a pass-through entity) is that you can take advantage of the TCJA (Tax Cuts and Jobs Act of 2017). This legislation allows business owners to claim a 20% deduction on qualified business income. As long as you and your spouse make under $415,000 a year (or you yourself make under $207,500) you can deduct 20% of your business income from taxes. If you make more than $415,000 a year, you won't get those tax benefits, but also congratulations on successfully building a micro-agency![7]

It helps if you start bookkeeping and treating your business like a business from day one. If you aren't great at accounting, you need to either get a business partner who is, or you need to get great at it. It's not enough to trust an uninvested bookkeeper or CPA. *You* need to understand what is happening with the agency's money.

I have consulted with so many potential agency owners (and already-owners who are struggling with the process) who dismiss the importance of being intimately involved with their own financial process. From day one, they hire a CPA and don't look at their own expenses or revenue ever again.

Here's the thing: CPAs are great for taxes and record-keeping,

---

[7] The tax code changes faster than I can keep up with it. Specific numbers change every year due to inflation. Treat these numbers as vague waving-in-the-wind.

but they are not business consultants or advisors. They're not going to tell you that you spent too much on marketing last month, or that you need to think longer-term about your cost per acquisition, or that you need to spend *more* on marketing. They're just there to balance your checkbook and keep your records looking pretty, and help you file tax returns at the end of the year.

In a previous chapter I mentioned how technical agencies tend to do better financially than creative agencies. There is a reason that creative agencies rarely do well from a numbers basis, and it's not just because creative work pays less than technical work. It also has to do with the business proficiency of the principal.

Creative folks stereotypically don't care as much about the money side of things as the technical folks (and I say this as a former creative). I've seen so many creative agencies flounder simply because they focus on creative work and creative output more than bringing in income. What is so shortsighted about this is the fact that many times, bringing in boring revenue is what actually funds the creative work and keeps the agency afloat.

If you are a creative, consider taking a little bitter pill of hard advice right now. *Get better at the stuff you'd rather avoid.* Which is, usually, things like accounting and legal structure and sales. You may have wanted to start your own business so you have creative freedom without oppressive corporate influences, but what will allow you to continue to work for yourself is a mastery of the revenues and expenses your newly founded agency is providing.

And for the technical types, there's an equal opposite truth that is sometimes hard to swallow: *not everything can be quantified.*

Branding, content creation, customer service, video campaigns, lots of critical elements to running an agency can simply seem like unjustified expenses. That doesn't mean they actually are unjustified, it just means they can be hard to attribute success towards.

THE BEAUTY OF TAKING RESPONSIBILITY

One of the greatest things about running an agency is that you are responsible for it. That can either be very scary, or very fulfilling. (We all make mistakes, of course, and taking responsibility for those is important as well).

However, your success as an agency can be built upon and scaled in ways that in-house or freelance roles can't.

Perhaps you've worked in the corporate world before. If so, you've experienced the politics and interpersonal maneuvering that comes along with office life. At a previous position I was the director of special projects — essentially tasked with developing and testing new marketing concepts for the company to try.

One of my big projects was launching crypto adoption: even in my initial job interview, I had pitched the idea of being the first within the industry to accept Bitcoin as payment. It took a lot of work to get this going, mostly because of the internal approval process and getting the various stakeholders of different departments to get on board.

But once it was launched, I knew it was time to take advantage of the crypto support. I did some digital PR outreach, knowing it would also help our SEO traffic.

For a myriad of reasons, the company was going through some hard times. Increasing sales was vital to the survival of the company (thus my position testing new marketing concepts, I suppose). I had a meeting with some of the leadership to discuss, and somewhat surprisingly I found myself on the critiqued end of the table.

"We aren't being proactive enough in our marketing," the CEO said. "There are ways to get exposure that don't cost, so I'd like you to do more of that. Look at this," he said, pulling up his browser. "We're on this popular list of companies that accept crypto! Why can't you do this? If you could do free marketing like this, we'd be meeting more of our KPIs."

"Well...I *did* do that," I replied. "I emailed the author of that list and got us on it."

It was at that moment I realized two things: first, in a corporate setting I needed to document and amplify my own work, otherwise I'd disappear in a swamp of anonymity, and second, when you're working for someone else, you can never take total responsibility for the good *or* the bad.

Running an agency allows you to do both.

You can reap the rewards without limit, even if you have to take credit for failures every once in a while as well.

COFOUNDER OR SOLO?

At some point, you will need to ask yourself if you're going to be the sole founder of your new agency, or if you're going to bring a co-founder on board.

Successful agencies can run both ways. I know and respect

some amazingly talented solo owners, and I also know plenty of great micro-agencies owned by two or three people.

There are upsides and downsides to both, but in general it really comes down to complementary skillsets — and above all, absolute trust.

It's worth noting that the Discosloth micro-agency model doesn't really work well if it's just you, and no one else (that's called freelancing). The micro-agency model requires a certain level of volume that simply can't be fulfilled by one person alone. A freelancer can perhaps support a dozen smaller or medium-sized clients at once, and there is so much time spent in fulfillment that scaling further is nearly impossible. The work becomes unbearable (rare is the person who can do actual work, do sales, contribute to the community of your industry, do customer service, do accounting, invoice, and brand yourself at the same time while gaining more and better clients).

So you're either going to have to start with a partner, or hire someone right off the bat. Either works.

Hiring or partnering with someone just like you may feel natural, but it's a bad idea. And this is where it's highly counter-intuitive. I've seen agencies start up which are comprised of three or four highly skilled, highly intelligent people, but they are too alike. An agency comprised solely of creatives is destined to fail, just like an agency comprised solely of spreadsheet warriors is destined to fail. You have to have the math and the art; the yin and the yang; the black and the white; the money and the ideas.

Likewise, you've got to have absolute trust. At Discosloth we are lucky, since we're a married couple (I suppose some folks don't trust their spouses, but that's another issue altogether).

Once I was chatting with a fellow who was starting up an agency with an acquaintance. He was asking me what was the best way to structure the legal partnership, how to make sure the partner didn't have unfettered access to the company funds, how to legally ensure the partner would support their fair share of the workload, how to make sure the partner wasn't going to steal all the clients and take the business on the side. This guy was going into this agency partnership with no trust, total paranoia, and a strictly transactional, eye-for-an-eye approach.[8]

A single phrase popped into my mind: "live by the sword, die by the sword".

If you start a business thinking you're going to get screwed by your co-founder, you shouldn't be going into business with them. This is not to say that there isn't a time and place to set up your company properly, and make sure your ducks are in order. But if you approach everything in life as a matter of future litigation, you're going to live a life of suits, counter-suits, and paranoia.

---

[8] A rule of thumb I've always gone by is: would you trust your business partner with your bank password? If not, why are you even partnering with them?

Chapter Takeaways

....

1. Starting an agency means you have to take responsibility for the failures as well as the successes. Which potential failures are you most worried about, and how can you proactively prevent these?

2. How much savings do you have, and how long can you survive without positive cashflow?

3. Everyone has aspects of running a business that they're less skilled at. Which aspects are you most deficient in?

4. Are you going to start this agency on your own, or are you finding a co-founder? Do they have the same skillset as you, or is it complementary?

5. Do you trust your co-founder?

GETTING LEADS

"Just what is it that you want to do? We wanna get loaded and we wanna have a good time." — Primal Scream, Loaded

Getting leads is the most important factor in any digital agency.

Hands down.

No question about it.

If your agency has conquered this summit, there is no limitation to where you can take your company. It is single-handedly the most make-it-or-break-it aspect of a successful agency. By far, getting leads is the topic people have asked me the most.

I don't have a single method per se of getting leads, but I do have quite a bit of experience — in both failing to get leads and succeeding to get leads — and as an agency we definitely ended up finding our niche.

Five years into our agency's lifetime, we are now able to get a steady stream of high-quality inbound inquiries from potential clients. Every month, we get at least fifteen to twenty inquiries alto-gether, and I'd say four to five of them are usually legitimately inter-esting and viable inquiries. Of those, we perhaps onboard one or two a month.

The good thing about such a steady stream of inbound leads is that it enables us to be progressively pickier about those with whom we work. It lets us have the luxury of moving forward only with people we *personally like*, which is sort of a hidden benefit. It's so much easier to work with people who you vibe with. You never have to dread picking up the phone if you legitimately like the person who's calling.

Our stream of leads has evolved over the years. During the first two years as a company, we actually got most of our leads from two sources: SEO forums, and Fiverr. A couple years in, after we'd published a book and lots of website marketing content, more of our leads started coming from readers or referrals. Meanwhile, we had been building up our personal brands on platforms across the internet, and more and more folks were finding us through our gen-eral interactions. And now, five years in, a surprising amount of our leads come from a source you'd never guess.

Our first secret weapon, starting in 2017, was Fiverr of all places. Fiverr is a gig platform where consumers can pay small amounts for professionals to complete tasks for them. We were lucky enough to start on Fiverr early on, when digital marketing was much less competitive on that platform, and became a Top Seller quickly, once we had passed the minimum threshold of $20,000 earned on the platform (that's a fairly easy threshold to pass if you are charging $500 for a setup). We set up another account and applied (and received) Fiverr Pro status, and this began working in tandem with our other account.

This was a secret weapon for us, and for an infant agency, it was critical. It gave us the cashflow to enter the PPC market, while building our brand. Most people did not believe it was possible to gain success on such a "cheap" platform. And, to be sure, Fiverr has never had a great reputation. Fortunately, it wasn't too hard to stand out. A few hundred five star reviews was all it took to get a steady stream of multiple setups per week. Surprisingly, we landed some extremely fantastic long-term clients from Fiverr, with whom we work to this day — including accounts that spend millions on Google Ads per year.

Unfortunately, Fiverr had an IPO, went public, and took a turn for the worse. These days it is mostly full of spam and low-quality providers that have clogged up the platform, and over the course of the last few years we have lost interest. It's giving us diminishing returns.

Around the same time as Fiverr's decline, luckily, our branding and authority within our domain of PPC began to rise, and we started to get many more referrals and inquiries from folks who found us organically.

Meanwhile, we had been building up our social accounts on several platforms for years. I regularly engaged with the PPC communities on Twitter, Reddit, and LinkedIn, and over five years had made some good friends within the industry. Our stream of leads from online communities grew massively. For example, within our

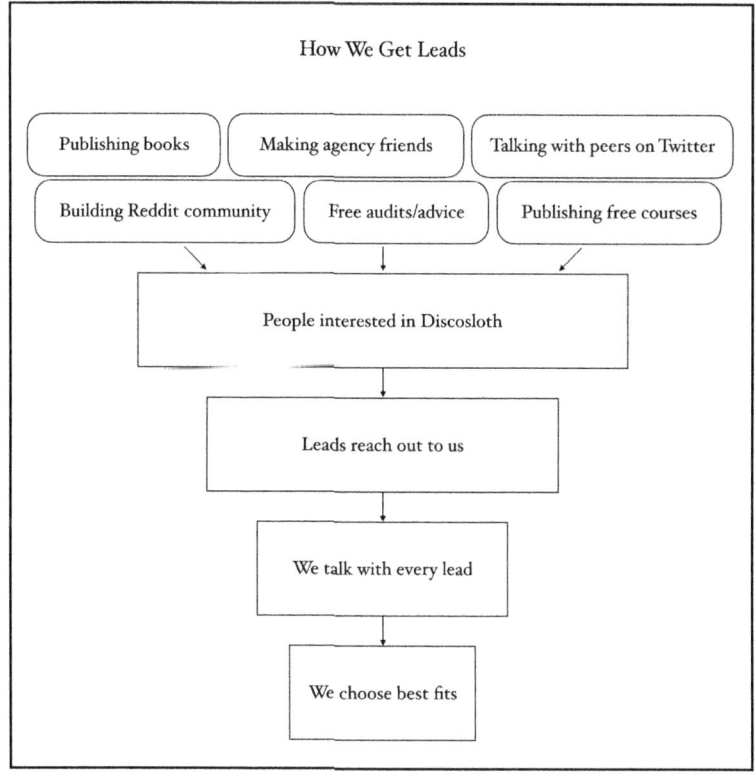

first six months of engaging on Reddit, we onboarded well over six figures of revenue from Reddit alone.

The strategy I used on Reddit was totally unorthodox, something that I haven't seen many other folks execute in the same manner.

Reddit, in general, is a toxic place full of anonymous accounts, master trolls, and overall snark. I decided to create a personal brand upon Reddit that was contrary to everything normally on Reddit.

I posted under my real name. I wrote carefully crafted, detailed, polite responses to questions about paid search and digital marketing in general. I never linked to our own website or even pitched our services. I gave away a lot of knowledge and insight for free, and spent hours spreading as much value and "insider knowledge" as humanly possible. I didn't dunk on newcomers or people with silly questions. I wrote long and carefully researched answers. I helped competitors who were having problems with their agencies.

The result was an incredible amount of positive response. I started a small subreddit, which gained in popularity, and got a steady stream of incoming inquiries from people who wanted us to help them with their advertising.

And during all of this, I never linked to our own website, and not once ever pitched our services. No spam whatsoever...so I only got legitimately interested individuals who wanted to learn more about our Google Ads process.

This was counter to most of the digital marketer activity I saw other folks engage in on Reddit, which was a lot of self-promotion or ego-swinging. It was incredible the impact that simply behaving helpfully and professionally made upon our brand.

It may seem risky giving away our secret for building our brand on Reddit...but if it means that folks start being a little nicer on that platform, I'll take the loss.

STAYING IN THE GAME

The hardest part about building a brand through content is keeping on doing it.

Diligence goes a long way. Building a funnel of inbound leads through domain expertise is not something that will give you results in a week, or a month, or even six months. It's something that will bring you results *years* from now.

As long as you can make it during this long ramp-up process, the work will pay off eventually.

Since there is such a long lag in between starting your content creation strategy, and getting actual results, this means that the vast majority of your competitors will give up. Even the most dedicated writers, speakers, and video producers will get tired of creating all this content after a year or two. It's understandable. Why spend so much time and energy on something when you can't see any measurable results?

The thing is, the more you do something, the better you become at it, and the more sheer volume of content you have created exists out there in the digital ether.

It can be daunting. It can be outright discouraging, for that matter. But I don't think there is a single successful authority out there who wishes they started later. If anything, I think every single one of us regrets not starting sooner. Sometimes I think about the date I actually started building things online, and really wish I'd stuck with a few of those projects.

I built my first website in 2003, and started engaging in various digital communities as an awkward, clueless teenager around the same time.

If I had maintained the same project since then...can you imagine the benefit I'd have reaped by running something for a solid 19 years? That's centuries in internet time. That's more than half the age of the popular internet itself.

Staying the course is important. You will get better and better at explaining, understanding, writing, talking, and selling what you do.

But don't expect to reap the results until years later...perhaps a few years later.

Time and dedication are the only true barriers to entry.

*Since 2017, our agency has maintained an average of 24 clients on retainer each month. It's interesting that our revenue has more than quadrupled over the same period. We have had a focus on getting **better** clients, not **more** clients.*

Chapter Takeaways

1. From the moment you start your agency, how long can you survive without revenue? Three months, six months, a year?

2. Can you utilize your existing network (professional acquaintances, colleagues, clients, friends, family) to gain clients? Or will you have to start from scratch?

3. Do you have a short-term method to gain leads while you build up your long-term brand approach to gaining leads?

SELLING TO CLIENTS

"Only the meek get pinched. The bold survive." — Ferris Bueller

Sales.

People hate it.

But if you don't do it, your agency ain't gonna be around much longer.

I never ever really wanted to *sell* anything, which is probably why I went to college for visual media design and thought I was going to be a filmmaker. Then, life hit me and I realized that not only did I need to be able to pay rent every month, but that maybe one day I wanted to drive a car made more recently than 1984 (my daily driver for seven years was an '84 Mercedes 300D — which had over a quarter million miles on the odometer before it stopped counting).

Eventually I started *selling* — and at the same time, not coincidentally, I started making money.

Eventually, I also acquired some newer & nicer wheels, too (everyone has their motivations and vices)!

The thing that always stuck with me, however, was my intrinsic dislike of hard sales. And to this day, I don't think I've actually ever hard-sold anything.

The hustle and sales-bro grind has always been a bit distasteful to me. I'm not interesting in pushing anybody, or having a strict process of selling to anyone, or really having to convince anyone of anything. I'd rather lead by example, contribute value for free, and have people start off our relationship by *wanting* to pay Discosloth for our expertise.

At Discosloth, we don't cold-call. We don't do pitches. We don't respond to RFPs. We literally expend *no time and energy* in catering to relationships that don't already exist in some manner.

That's not to say the hard sales method doesn't work. Some folks are great at cold calls, pitching, grant writing, sending proposals, and time-intensive negotiations. If that is you, that's great. Do your thing. It's just not something we have ever done, or been interested in doing.

INCOMING IS BETTER THAN OUTGOING

Instead of reaching out to potential clients, we prefer to accommodate inbound inquiries.

The reason?

If someone comes to *us*, they are massively more likely to sign on than someone to whom we have first reached out. They're pre-filtered. They are already interested. They already know who we are. They want help...not just from anyone, but from *us*. They've done the legwork, they're already sold, and they think we can help them.

The "sales process" in this case is hardly even a sales process. It's more of a filtering process, wherein I make sure we can truly help them — and if they have any doubts, I can either assure them that every contingency really is covered, or I can see that we might not be the greatest fit after all.

Here is what a sales process for a typical customer looks like for Discosloth.

First, they will have found us via referral or, most likely, having read something that either Anya or I wrote. They have usually either read one of our books, or come across some of my PPC content on Reddit. These are typically people who are in charge of their company's marketing department, or who perhaps own a small business and do a lot of their own work. Sometimes, they are currently contracting with another agency but are unhappy with the work.

They will then do a little research. They head to Google, (handily, the platform of our expertise) and search for my name. They probably find my personal website and get a sense of who I am, personally. They see that I've traveled a lot, I like old cars, and that I have contrarian opinions on small business, alternative investments, and science fiction (*Star Wars* sucks, *Star Trek* rules). If that hasn't somehow soured them on the idea yet, they'll then search for Discosloth, and find our website (as you can imagine, we pretty much dominate the search results for our company name... not a lot of competition there). After reading through our site, visiting our About page, and realizing we are a real company with real faces...if they like what they see, they'll send us an email.

I try to respond to every contact form submission within a few hours, or at the very most within 24 hours. There is a real and noticeable difference in potential lead interest the sooner I respond to an inquiry. Getting a response within a couple hours is impressive to leads, and they are usually very excited to hear back so quickly (this says more about the total lack of organization or customer service in today's world, than anything about my response time).

If they haven't already given me enough info in the initial contact form, I'll ask them a few questions about budget, geographical targeting, campaign goals, and any other questions. Many times I can immediately tell that we won't be a great fit, and I'll let them know politely that we probably aren't the best agency fit for them. If they do seem like a potential fit, I'll do my own Google research on *them*. I'll look up the person, their LinkedIn, their company, and look for reviews or external feedback on the company. Within a couple minutes, I can usually tell if this is worth pursuing. We schedule a brief phone call or a Zoom meeting. I like to keep the first call within 15 to 30 minutes in length.

The purpose of this initial phone call is not for gathering data, or discovery, or really anything tangible at all. It's literally to see if I like talking to this person. Because, if I like talking to *them*, usually they like talking to *me*.

We chat about cars. Or traveling. Or coffee. Or literally any sort of common interest we share. I ask about their business, issues they're struggling with, I share any anecdotal experience we have with the vertical, and I wrap it up by telling them that I'll send a follow-up email with my thoughts.

Instinct usually works. But not always. I'm often wrong. One time, I had a quick phone call from an agency owner that desperately needed help scaling his PPC services, and was interested in engaging us for some white label work[9]. Although my gut said the engagement may not be a great fit (and by now, you'd think I'd know that I should usually trust my gut), the fellow was incredibly respectful and professional, and I felt obligated to give him an hour of my time at the very least. So I hopped on a video call to talk to him.

The guy was pleasant and professional, no doubt about it. But he had some expectations that I can only imagine came from decades embedded into the traditional marketing world. On our call, he asked if I was going to *present*.

"Present?" I asked.

"Yes, do you have a Powerpoint, or a pitch deck you are going to share? I would love to see your case studies and your services proposal?"

I realized then and there that the expectations were totally misaligned, and I doubted that misunderstandings would end here. This fellow had emailed multiple times and we'd already had a brief phone call, so he *really* wanted Discosloth to help his agency. I explained that we don't have a pitch deck, and I don't want to convince anyone to work with us if they don't want to. I'm here to answer questions and offer some free advice on his current situation. I even offered some quick help with some account access issues he

---

[9] As an aside, white-label work for traditional agencies is a great way to get some ongoing revenue, while not having to deal with account management!

was having.

He appreciated the help...but he did *not* understand. I could see the gears turning in his head.

I get it. Traditional advertising agencies thrive through a never ending process of RFPs and pitch decks and proposals that take weeks to create. I can imagine it's hard to break out of that mold.

But here he was, desperately needing some help, and after coming across some of our PPC-related content online, he knew we had expertise...and he *really wanted us to help*. What exactly am I supposed to pitch?

The benefit of developing a brand, and helping folks directly as a form of sales process, is that you don't have to pitch. There's nothing to convince anybody of. They already want you.

RELATIONAL OVER TRANSACTIONAL

Here's my secret about sales.

It's how I, an introvert and low-keyed person all round, can manage to keep my sanity.

Sales is not about numbers. It's not about contracts. It's not about negotiations. It's about *relationships* — and how much that person (the client) likes us (Discosloth, or myself in particular).

As a matter of fact, this is an important cultural business approach that many folks miss. It throws off many agency owners who are trying to make sales. I've gotten some pushback from fellow agency owners on this, but based upon the agency owners I know are killing it, I'm convinced relationship-based sales is a critical factor in sales success.

When the conversation is too metric-driven, or negotiation-driven, or contract-driven, or performance-guarantee-driven, this is a red flag that the client will not be invested in our agency for the long run. They will not have patience for A/B testing, campaign experimentation, or our slow & steady process of scaling a Google Ads account. They aren't around for the long-term. The instant something happens (seasonal fluctuation, for example) they'll jump ship.

When the conversation is merely about what we can deliver, and at what price, there is no relationship. It's transactional rather than relational.

While this works for some people, it doesn't work for us. Our primary goal is our customer's ROI...but this is a goal we can only reach if we have our customer's trust. If they can't trust us, they will inevitably micro-manage the campaign in order to reach those numbers sooner. In our view, there is no point in paying Discosloth to help achieve these numbers if we can't make full use of our expertise. That's why trust — and relationships rather than transactions — is so important for our sales process.

More than a few times, I've been chatting with some agency owners who have expressed difficulty with their sales process. Their question has almost always been worded the same: "How do you convince so-and-so that they need to invest in marketing?"

My answer: you *don't*.

Spending time and energy convincing someone that they need your service is not very efficient. You're going to get clients that A) aren't super interested in your service, B) aren't going to invest a whole lot into it, and C) will jump ship the first time they feel friction. Your time and energy will be vastly better spent on finding folks who already need your service and are ready to pull the trigger.

Sure, the number of folks out there who are actively looking for your service is probably a fraction of all possible clients — but I'd rather have *one* super-interested, super-invested client than have a dozen uninterested, uninvested clients.

That's why the cold-calling game can be so exhausting (and difficult to scale) for the beginning micro-agency. Yes, there are lots of small business owners in any location. No, not all of them are interested in your services, not all of them need your services, and not all of them are even going to like you enough to work with you.

That's the massive benefit of creating a brand and making it easy for *interested* people to find you. Generating content, providing value, and proving your expertise — even before a potential lead picks up the phone to contact you — is one of the most efficient and scalable ways to make sales easy. This doesn't just make it easy, it makes it *natural*.

GIVING TREMENDOUS VALUE...FOR FREE

When someone calls you, they are probably familiar with who you are, and want to explore working with you, but they rarely *know* you're the right pick. They may have heard great things, but everybody wants a little proof that you know what you're talking about.

That is why I try to give as much up-front value, no strings attached, as humanly possible.

This can be as general as basic bird's-eye-view strategy advice, or as specific as diving into a potential lead's Google Analytics account and identifying conversion errors. If a potential lead's business model and personal rapport really impress me, and I really want to land this client, we go to a great deal of effort in order to impress them. Often, we'll essentially do a mini-audit of their account for free, and tell them the exact things we would do right off the bat to help them improve their results.

The interesting thing is, there are agency owners out there who really have a dislike for this approach. I have been told, in no uncertain terms, that this practice of offering free advice "cheapens the industry" and that I should be charging hourly for my knowledge. Apparently, giving info away for free hurts everyone else in the industry by setting the wrong expectations.

I couldn't disagree more.

Here's the thing: we are *not* working for free. That's an incredibly shortsighted complaint, because there have been several instances where we have won clients over because of the amount of advice we gave up front, with no strings attached.

In one notable instance, the marketing head of an extremely large brand (you have probably used their products) approached us and asked if we could look at their Google Ads campaigns. This brand was planning on spending $3.2 million on Google Ads over the next year.

Of course I said yes. I not only said yes — we dropped everything and spent several hours putting together a moderately detailed analysis of their current situation, and identified immediate changes we could make to improve their results. We showed them some structural issues and gave them an idea of what our first few months would look like. It wasn't a full-on audit, but it was just a very thorough account analysis.

They signed on — and afterwards, the marketing lead told me that he had been in talks with a competing PPC agency, but they refused to even look at his campaign unless he paid them for an hour of consulting.

I wish I could help every agency avoid this sort of short-term thinking. Discosloth worked for "free" for two hours...and then on-boarded a multi-million dollar client the next day. If that cheapens the industry, then so be it. I will take the revenue, and I hope you would too.

The reason that providing tremendous value is so important is that *you are competing in a field of millions*. If any agency — and I mean *any* agency — thinks that they are special enough to just stand out from the crowd by their own skills and virtue alone, then they are wielding a unique form of ego and arrogance that is only going to end in bankruptcy and embarrassment. Remember that until you have actually developed a relationship with a client, you're untested. Your reputation is all that precedes you — not your results, not yet!

If you think your methods, your designs, and your strategies are so exclusive, proprietary, and special, you should go into rocket science.

Giving away free advice doesn't mean you have to labor in abject poverty, but you have to do *something* to get your foot in the door with the companies you would love to work with. If that means doing some free or discounted work, or providing some insightful strategies or actionable ideas — then *just do it*.

Chapter Takeaways

....

1. Are you going to take a hard-sales (proactive) approach to gaining clients for your agency, or a soft-sales (reactive) approach to gaining clients?

2. What domain expertise can you provide for free? In what medium could you publish this expertise?

3. In the sustainable micro-agency model, you want to spend your time making it easier for people interested in your service to find *you*, instead of spending your time finding *them*. How can you increase your agency's visibility in your niche?

ONBOARDING & MANAGING CLIENTS

So you've made the sale.

You've convinced your client lead that you're the right agency for the job. They want to know next steps.

What do you send them? What information do you need to know? What do you need them to do?

ACCUMULATE INFO

As a paid search agency, our primary metric for success is ROI. We literally only exist as a business in order to make profit for our clients. They pay us good money because we make them good money.

Therefore, the most important information you need from your client is information about their business model, their profit margins, their goals, their budgets, and their targeting.

The exact information you request from your new client will vary based upon your services and your client's business, but in general you'll want to know how much their profit per sale is (in other words, how much $ value they put on a conversion) and what they consider to be a qualified lead or sale.

You'll want to know how much they need to spend on this marketing project (including your fee, your expenses, ad spend or equipment costs, etc), who their audience is, and other lead or sale-based factors.

You'll want access to everything you need to do your job (this may be Google Analytics, WooCommerce, Google Ads, Facebook Ads Manager, LinkedIn Ads, Shopify, you name it).

You'll also want to send them an invoice and get that paid. We'll talk more about pricing and payments in other chapters, but some level of up-front investment is important to ensure that your clients A) are invested in you and your project and B) actually have the money to pay you.

ANALYZE EXISTING PERFORMANCE

The benefit of being a niche agency, and focusing on one specific technical service, is that you've done it so many times that it takes you five minutes to know what's wrong with an account.

If you do SEO, you'll know right away where you need to be looking in order to identify common mistakes. Within a few minutes you'll be able to log into Search Console, do a PageSpeed test, run a Sitebulb report, and nearly instantly know how much work it'll be to turn this client's performance around.

A web developer will be able to quickly identify why a site is loading slowly: a couple clicks and visits to View Source, and he'll notice that each individual page on a website is actually a separate

WordPress installation (yes...one of our clients had this issue. They had over forty separate WordPress installations, one for each page).

For a PPC agency like Discosloth, having a specialty makes account analysis a breeze. All we need is access to Google Ads and Google Analytics. We start by looking at the current account performance of the current setup. We look at campaign structure, the type of campaigns clients are using, the keyword match type (people use *way* too many broad keywords!) and we look at what type of traffic clients are getting and how it converts into sales. We also look at % of traffic coming from paid channels, versus other channels. If all the traffic is coming from paid channels, this indicates that the company has no real branding or external awareness, so ads are the only thing folks are using to make a purchase decision. We look at organic traffic, which usually indicates the company has been fairly successful for a while, and it'll be easier to convert searches into sales. In short, we can glance at a few elements and have an accurate idea of where a campaign is at.

We usually send our short analysis in an email format, communicated in a conversational manner. In an email or two, we can typically get a good grasp of what the client's goals are, what they're trying to improve, and then explain based on current data how much they can reasonably expect to grow through our PPC work.

SET REALISTIC EXPECTATIONS

If your goal is to keep clients a long time (and it should be) then don't make promises you can't keep. If you promise your client 10x returns in 1 month, just to be able to land the contract, well, that's not a contract you're going to keep.

You may land the client, but big promises can rarely be delivered. This means that 1) you're going to lose the client and 2) the client will complain about you, not recommend you to anyone, and maybe even find somewhere to write a poor review.

After you analyze your future client's performance, set realistic expectations: expectations that you *know* you can provide. Tell them how it can take months to achieve certain goals.

It's fine if you undersell your results. If you exceed these undersold expectations, you'll have a happy client with a happy business. If your client wants 10x results *now*, resist the impulse to say you can do it. You're probably not a good fit, and I can assure you that it will be a nightmare working with them.

BAD FIT CLIENTS

As a rule, I don't like trash-talking clients. Very rarely is any client a bad client. Mostly, when you run into issues, you just have a bad fit. It doesn't mean they're terrible in general — they may just be terrible *for you*.

Of course, every once in a while you do get a truly surprising, wonderfully rotten bad apple, but thankfully those are few and far between.

There are many reasons that a client turns out to be a poor fit for your agency. And despite all the preventative work you do during discovery, sometimes you just can't know beforehand. We all make mistakes, including onboarding clients that we shouldn't have.

There's no question, however, that you must weed out the bad ones. It may sound counter intuitive, but poor-fit clients prevent you from growing. It has to be done. It's harder to do so at first, but as your agency grows and evolves, so does your threshold for fit.

Chapter Takeaways

1. For your specific niche, what sort of onboarding information will you need to collect from each potential customer?

2. In your niche, what sort of expectations can you set upfront? How can you under-promise and over-deliver?

3. What specific elements define a "bad fit client" for you? How could you see your threshold evolving over time?

MANAGING FULFILLMENT

"If you break little promises, you'll break big ones." - Cormac McCarthy[10]

When you first start a micro-agency, you're going to be the one doing all the work.

Unless, of course, you've got a fat startup budget from angel investors or VC or you sold a business or something...in which case, close this book and go make some more money!

Fulfillment is expensive unless you and your co-founder do it yourself, which is exactly what we did for the first couple years of Discosloth's history.

We were fortunate enough to have a good pairing of skills. Anya is extremely technical and proficient at a gamut of things from conversion tracking, Google Ads, analytics, organization — you name it. I'm good at copywriting, sales, branding, web design, and account management in general.

If you're partnering with someone to cofound your agency, find someone who has complementary skills to yours...someone who

---

[10] Cormac McCarthy, *The Road* (2006)

makes up for your flaws (Anya's organizational, accounting, and process skills have been our saving grace...you don't want to see a spreadsheet after I've hacked away at it). If you're doing solo fulfillment, it might be a bit harder, but it's entirely possible. I know a lot of guys who started their agency as a solo freelancer, and simply scaled beyond their own seat.

WHY QUALITY FULFILLMENT IS IMPORTANT

There are really just four possible approaches to agency work: high quantity/low quality, low quantity/high quality, high quantity/high quality, or low quantity/low quality.

The obvious one to avoid is low quantity/low quality. This is an agency that does bad work, and doesn't even have much of it either. These agencies pop up all the time, but they literally cannot sustain themselves. They pop up, and fold less than a year later. Bad work, no volume. Not a great combination.

The obvious one everyone would love to achieve is high quantity/high quality. Wouldn't you love to have hundreds of clients and deliver stellar, world-class work for all of them? The problem is that this is just really, really hard. It's hard enough getting clients. It's even harder doing good work. Combine the two, and you have the true unicorns of the agency world. It's possible...and those agencies *are* out there...but it's also improbable.

The two remaining approaches are high quantity/low quality and low quantity/high quality.

I would classify Discosloth's approach as low quantity/high quality, because we don't have a whole lot of volume, and in my biased opinion I think we do amazing work. However, we don't have what it takes to do amazing work on hundreds of clients...that's why we intentionally keep our client roster low, cap the amount of accounts that our specialists and managers handle, and are very picky about the sorts of new clients we onboard. We simply can't hire or scale fast enough to onboard lots of clients and still do the level of work we like to do. It's the approach I think that most profitable and sustainable micro-agencies need to aim for. Less clients, but better clients.

The most common approach of all is high quantity/low quality, and I'll take some time to address this approach as I see it all too often. The frustrating part about the high quantity/low quality agency is that it *does* bring revenue. So in the interest of fairness, I can't dismiss it offhand without giving it some serious consideration.

This an agency model focuses on massive intake, and deliverables by any means possible. It usually requires lots of outbound sales (email, LinkedIn, phone campaigns, advertising) in order to get the sheer amount of leads necessary to sustain the business. The model comes with downsides. First, you have to deliver all this work. If you onboard a hundred clients, you need the manpower to actually do the work. Second, the cost of acquisition is almost always high. Advertising campaigns, account executives, and outreach in general is not cheap. So the overall profit margins are low (although the overall revenue can be high enough that it's still quite profitable in dollar amounts). And third, low quality fulfillment almost always means a high rate of churn.

As an illustration, I'll reference a conversation I had with a young PPC account specialist who was working in a UK full-service agency. This agency was the most egregious example of high quantity/low quality work that I've ever seen.

The specialist said that this agency was the epitome of fast marketing, and it definitely was. He was managing 80 clients per week *and* doing the billing for them. Not only was he doing Google Ads, his specialty, but he was also doing SMS campaigns, Facebook Ads, graphic design, social media marketing, *and* reporting.

He was upset that he had fallen behind on some client billing, and the agency was upset that 8 of the clients hadn't paid that month. I couldn't really blame him. He had around 30 minutes per week, per client, to do all that?

I told him that he needed a better job (he agreed...and three weeks later got a job at a different agency for 2x the pay, managing only 3 accounts per month). And then, out of curiosity, I asked him what the client churn rate was at his current agency.

It was 40%. That's right...four out of ten clients canceled after the first month.

The level of funnel-stuffing advertising and outreach you have to do to keep up with that level of churn is insane. I really can't fathom how an agency can live like that.

The real problem isn't even in the model itself. It's in stability.

See, you can ostensibly create a high quantity/low quality agency where you churn through clients *and* churn through your employees, and still have a bit of a profit at the end of the month.

But what this agency approach doesn't account for are the black swan events. The instant something goes haywire (the economy, a specific industry, losing multiple clients at once) it is nearly impossible to keep going through a difficult month, much less a difficult quarter. When you are constantly having to fill your bucket of leads with fresh leads, what happens when it stops? You lose 40% of your existing clients, and along with it 40% of your revenue. There is no way you have that high of a profit margin, so you're forced to fire staff, cut advertising, and now you're in a mess of a situation.

It's not sustainable. Profit margin is critical. Keeping churn down is critical. And, in my opinion, doing good work is the most critical of all. It'll give you a reputation that brings you free leads for the rest of your agency's life.

That's not to say these agencies aren't out there. They are. They do make money. It's just the hardest and most ruthless way to make money that I've seen in the industry.

To quote the specialist again: *fast marketing is not good marketing.*

SOLO FULFILLMENT

You need to deliver work. That can be solo fulfillment (the agency founders doing it themselves, which is essentially freelancing), or it can be hiring out temporary work, or hiring full-time employees.

Solo fulfillment is hard. Both Anya and I, before we met while working at another company, had freelance stints of our own years before.

I can't stress enough, however: a solo agency is not an agency. That's called being a freelancer. Sometimes it's a freelancer who hires out other freelancers. But it is not the same.

It is entirely possible to be a very successful freelancer. You can literally make hundreds of thousands a year just being a freelancer. But that's what it is, and at the end of the day you are going to face the various limitations and restrictions that come with being a freelancer.

First among these is bandwidth. When you are doing every step, you're extremely limited to just how much you can handle. When you have to brand yourself, gather leads, make a sale, have strategy calls, do the implementation, provide customer service, invoice everyone, do your accounting, and pay your taxes at the end of the year, there's not a whole lot of room left for the scaling part. Scaling and improving your branding and leads is critical to nail down before you can scale and improve other things — like how much revenue you're making.

Second, you simply can't do everything perfectly. There isn't a single human in the world who is an expert at everything involved in running a successful business. The likelihood that you're an expert in sales, accounting, customer service, implementation, meetings, branding, and content creation is very slim. (And, I might mention, if you really *do* think you're an expert in all of those things, you may need a wake-up call from your delusions of grandeur).

Third, there is a very real difference between the sorts of clients and projects you're working on as a freelancer versus a legitimate multi-person agency. And not only the sorts of projects, but the number of those projects. If it's just you, stalwart captain of your solo ship, you're going to have a very hard time charging the sorts of prices that you could as an agency. Whether it's excusable or not, it's just the reality. If you go to most clients as a freelancer, and ask for a $6,000/mo flat fee, they'll laugh you out of the door and instead just hire someone full-time. However, clients won't think twice about hiring an agency for $6,000/mo.

I am not entirely sure why this is the case, but it is. I have some opinions (mostly I think it's centered around perception rather than anything else) but unless you are a freelancer with a massive following and extensive domain expertise, it's rare you can onboard those massive Fortune 500 clients with the accompanying consulting rates.

HIRING FREELANCERS

Almost every micro-agency will hire freelancers or contractors before they hire a full-time employee. We did the same, when we started having too much work for the two of us to fulfill.

Hiring freelancers is always attractive, but it is difficult for a few reasons.

First, expectations can be tough to manage. As an agency, of course you want your freelancer's attention...but they also need to make good money, and if they're any good, they're going to have plenty of other work that they need to focus on. If you want more of their attention, you'll need to pay them. And, increasingly, that is *not* cheap.

Freelancers are usually freelancers because of three possible reasons.

(I may be about to offend a swathe of freelancers, but don't mind me. I was a freelancer for five years, and I'm targeting my former self as much as anyone else).

Freelancers are usually freelancers because they are either wanting more independence (a good thing), they are wanting to make more money than an average employee (also a good thing) or because they simply aren't good enough to be an employee (not a good thing).

As a young freelancer myself, I was all of those things. This makes it very hard for agencies to successfully hire and depend upon freelancers as consistent fulfillment models. An agency doesn't own a freelancer. There is no expectation that the freelancer will want to stick around. Freelancers don't get paid vacation, solid full-time paychecks, or trips to your annual company retreat. And if they're *good*, they're *expensive*.

WHITE-LABELED AGENCY WORK

I have a love/hate relationship with the white label fulfillment model. I love it because we, ourselves, are a part of this system. We do a lot of white label work for traditional ad agencies who don't have solid technical or digital departments. When the ad agencies themselves are solid companies, we really like working with them. We become an embedded part of the team and we truly enjoy helping other companies fulfill things that otherwise they couldn't work with.

Unfortunately, I hate this model because it's easily misused. It often results in some very, very poor quality relationships. As an agency, we've had some disappointing story arcs with the wrong sort of white-label client, and it took us a few duds before we learned the hard way to heavily pre-filter our white label clients.

When a legitimate ad agency (or even an established freelancer in a specific niche) comes to us for white labeling work, we are more than happy to help. We're playing a critical part in implementing work that the agency or freelancer understands *needs* to happen — but also understands they don't know how to do it.

However — it seems like starting digital agencies is a thing that salesy hustlers do on an hourly basis. I assume that somewhere, somehow, one of those marketing gurus published a course on how to make six figures by starting a digital agency without doing any work yourself...and a lot of people must have bought it.

Our first few years, especially when we were thirsty for work, we took on a few of these guys before we got better at seeing through the wool. Unfortunately, it's just a recipe for disaster.

These guys would spin up an agency, cold call a thousand folks, promise some results, sign some contracts, and *then* try to find someone to fulfill their promises.

Think about it. If you are starting an agency, but can't implement anything...and don't really even know the details of what you're recommending...how can you knowledgeably and ethically sell the right service to your clients?

In every situation, we would almost inevitably start work on a campaign and then realize we were having to deliver results that were totally unrealistic. The clients would get upset at the new agency founder (after all, he had promised 200% return on ad spend within a month!) and then the agency founder would get upset at *us*.

We no longer accept white labeling work for companies that

aren't truly established and fully professional in all aspects of their business. It's just not worth it. And that's why I don't recommend that a new agency founder expect to outsource all the work. If you don't know your own industry, you're not going to last.

HIRING YOUR TEAM

I think there is a sweet spot for a profitable digital micro-agency. The profitable sweet spot is an agency comprised of 3-5 full-time colleagues, including the founder or founders.

We will get more into the economics of the sweet spot in a later chapter (specifically, talking more about the 5-50 Valley of Death) but the first step is hiring your first full-time employee.

Moving beyond ourselves and our freelancers and hiring our first full-time employee was the best business decision we ever made at Discosloth — of course after the decision to start the business in the first place. Having a full-time employee allowed us to delegate, start scaling, and diversify our client base. All of these things (delegation, scaling, and diversification) were important and crucial steps towards increasing revenue.

We'll cover hiring full-time employees in a chapter of it's own. It's extremely difficult, but one of the most important things you'll ever do for your business.

I'll be entirely upfront about this. I'm not the right person to write this section. At Discosloth, we have hired great full-time employees — and at previous positions in other companies, we've hired folks into teams as well.

However, I think I've just gotten extremely lucky with our Discosloth team. I'd be doing you, the reader, a disservice if I don't admit that I have no idea what I'm doing when I'm hiring. It's just a gut thing, and it's been accurate so far.

The benefit, however, is that with the micro-agency model *you don't have to hire a lot*. That's sort of the entire point about keeping your overhead low and your revenue high.

A team can be built with freelancers, with part-time employees, by outsourcing all of the work, or by hiring full-time employees. I'll try to go over all of the options and bounce around the positives and negatives of each. We'll start with looking at hiring freelancers.

FREELANCERS

At the beginning, it's going to be financially difficult to hire full-time employees. We couldn't have done that during our first couple years.

Hiring freelancers is the only means of scaling at that point. I'm often asked by burgeoning new agency owners how they can develop an entire agency simply through freelancers, but I think it's an unsustainable model. Here's why.

With freelancers, you will find yourself paying per project, or per account. This works when you have three or four accounts, but what about when you get to twenty accounts? You will rapidly find that your margins are nonexistent.

With freelancers, you also have little say over your business model. Freelancers work for themselves, and they're not obligated to take on any account you throw at them. They can take off whenever they want, they can pretty much do work however they want, and that's their right. It's why they're a freelancer, and not an employee at an agency!

Although freelancers are definitely a valuable asset in many cases, they are best utilized when you're just starting out, or when you're so large you don't have the physical or time capacity to onboard and train new full-time employees.

The micro-agency, the sort we've worked on building, will find it difficult to scale with freelancers. Quality control is important, high cash margins are important, and taking the big step of hiring full-time team members will pay off in the end.

It's worth noting: you get what you pay for. A quality freelancer will be expensive. If you are approaching hiring freelancers because you think they'll be cheaper, you are going to be disappointed. Don't pay a freelancer a hundred bucks because you think it's what they're worth. You will get exactly what you pay for.

There are times to use freelancers (sometimes you just need extra help, now!) but expect to pay them a lot for their valuable insight — not treat them like cheap disposable labor that can be used like a baby wipe.

OFFSHORING & OUTSOURCING

When we started Discosloth, *we* were technically offshore ourselves. For the first two years, as a matter of fact, we were what has been termed "digital nomads", living for a few months each in Romania, Italy, Poland, Russia, and Mexico, before finally settling down back in the US. Our team now is scattered between the US and Europe.

"Offshoring", however, usually has more of a pejorative sense and is associated with terrible call center customer service or cheap, low-quality grunt work found on platforms like UpWork or Fiverr. And there is definitely a huge negative element in offshoring certain work, especially if the primary motive for offshoring is just to save money.

I encourage folks to view offshoring as less of a money-saving strategy, and more of a talent-attracting strategy.

Say for example you're located in Lubbock, Texas. Your agency is doing well, and you want to hire some additional help with paid search campaigns. You're going to have to find some experts to come into the office.

What is the likelihood that you're going to be able to find the perfect PPC specialist within commuting distance of Lubbock? First off, there's not all that many folks who are really into PPC. Second, they need to be good at what they do. Third, they need to be a good personal fit for your company. Fourth, they need to be looking for work and you need to be able to afford them. I could go on.

The good news is, today the recruiting net can be cast across the entire world. You don't have to settle anymore. And this allows your company to be tighter, more efficient, more specialized, and more profitable.

HIRING FULL-TIME EMPLOYEES

When we hired our first specialist, it was not easy. It took us around three months...and this was *before* the explosion of remote work, which would doubtless have made it even more difficult to find the perfect candidate.

We thought, at first, it would be easy to find who we needed. We're a remote company, so we have the entire world at our disposal, right? As it turns out, this made it harder rather than easier. We were competing with companies across the world for a very specific skillset. We tried all of the channels we could think of: specialized job boards, traditional job postings, inquiries within our personal networks.

The job board postings brought us less than stellar results. We were looking for an entry-level Google Ads specialist, which doesn't sound like too difficult of a role to fill. And it's a tech-focused marketing role, which is perfectly suited for remote work. The variety of applicants, however, was wildly confusing and overwhelming. Over 300 applicants applied during the first week.

We had an application from a fellow in California who made his salary demand up-front in his cover letter. I appreciated the initiative, but his cover letter also detailed how he would be working and structuring his work day, and he demanded $182,000 a year for a clearly entry-level job. Unfortunately, I had to take a hard pass on that one, and that was actually one of the better ones.

The worst part is that out of these hundreds of applicants, only four or five were actually relevant. We looked at the resumes of a pharmacist in Hawaii, a grocery store cashier in Ohio, an insurance salesman in Kansas, and everyone else from interior designers, telemarketers, professors, and landscapers.

After weeks of fruitless work, I decided we'd need to hire manually. Off to LinkedIn I went, and painstakingly searched for candidates who were as close to what we needed as possible. I narrowed the entire world down to around forty potential candidates, and sent a personal message to each. Only five responded. Three were not interested, one was actively looking for a job, and one already had a job but might be interested.

The first candidate, the one who was looking for a job, showed up at the first virtual interview and announced that she'd already accepted a job, but she'd appreciate an offer anyway. I didn't feel like indulging her, since she just wanted to negotiate her salary at her new job. The next offer was a perfect fit: so we poached her from her current agency, and she has been an excellent fit for the past several years.

That's the process of hiring that we first experienced, and it hasn't changed much since. New, small micro-agencies have to be extremely picky about full-time hiring, especially since salaries will be the largest part of your capital expenditure. Not to mention that a full-time team member is a direct reflection of your agency's skill, culture, speciality, and vibe. You want that to be perfect, and it's a tall order to fill.

Expect to spend weeks, if not months, finding the appropriate candidates for the job...especially if you're hiring for a critical technical role.

Chapter Takeaways

....

1. If you are partnering with a co-founder, you'll probably have a longer time before you need to hire your first employee. Do you have complementary skillsets to bide you over while you find the perfect fit?

2. At what volume of work can you no longer fulfill by yourself, and what revenue level do you need to be at before making your first full-time hire?

3. How much does your profit margin reduce if you have to hire freelancers to fulfill your workload?

ORGANIZATION AND PROCESS

"Simplicity is the ultimate sophistication." – Leonardo Da Vinci[11]

I've never been a fan of overly structured business processes... likely, because I've never had to work in a massive corporation. From day one of my career, I've worked in small business. Anya spent some time working in a multi-national, but she'll be the first to admit that she hated it, and shifted to working at small businesses and startups as soon as possible.

My first real job out of college was in a startup of 20 or so employees. I freelanced for years after this, and scribbles on a yellow legal pad is about as close as I ever got to being organized. My second real job was for a luxury airfare company (that functioned much like a startup, except it was thirty years old) and yet it never had more than 50 employees. The reality of working in small companies is that the team you're working with is even smaller — usually a group of three to four folks at most. There's very little need for complicated organizational processes at this size. But there *is* a need

---

[11] Leonardo da Vinci, *The Da Vinci Notebook*

for *something.*

PROJECT TRACKING

When we first started Discosloth, we didn't need organization...there was just two of us, so we just used spreadsheets. Turns out, you don't need a fancy CRM or sales process when you're just doing a few account setups here and there.

Once we started hiring, we quickly realized that we needed to get our organizational ducks in a row (and thanks to our first employee, who kindly requested that we figure *something* out). After looking at the options, we landed on a simple and straightforward workflow that easily enabled everyone involved in a project to keep tabs on status.

We use Trello to run our project management process, but any similar software will work well. We like Trello because it's simple, and additionally we like the kanban approach (card-based tasks which can be sorted into different stacks of priority or completion status).

We're remote at Discosloth, so we function as a virtual team. That means that asynchronous written communication is almost always preferable to vocal or in-person chats, when it comes to project management. We use email extensively, both for external client communication and internal communication. Outside of these, we use Trello and chat to work out quick issues. As the "external" account face, I typically translate client requests into Trello cards or emails.

We have one weekly internal Zoom meeting discussing the

state of everything. We talk about current projects, client performance, and discuss what we need to focus on next. Everything else is usually communicated through email, chat, or Trello.

FINANCIAL TRACKING

We use a yearly spreadsheet for our business accounting. In our spreadsheet, we have individual sheets for each month containing all the invoices we need to send, all the payments we need to make, and we update everything in real time as soon as it's been paid.

This way, we can easily keep track of how much we'll be making and spending each month, we can see how long it takes a client to pay, and we can get a bird's-eye-view of upcoming expenses in the next period.

We also keep a sheet with how much we've made every single month from when we started, along with a little graph showing the growth. This helps us visualize our trajectory, puts things in a long-term perspective, and helps us remain optimistic when we sometimes have a low month (overall, the graph goes up and to the right!)

We use Quickbooks for our more accurate, detailed bookkeeping which is updated every month. This helps us estimate our taxes and gives us the exact dollar amounts with which our business operates.

Chapter Takeaways

....

1. Do you have the technical skills to do your own bookkeeping and accounting, or do you plan on outsourcing that?

2. Most agencies can use a simple spreadsheet to run project tracking at the beginning. Once you hire and need to scale, what software or processes do you plan on using?

REPORTING & ANALYTICS

The state of reporting is dismal.

I'm not just talking about journalism — although I think most of us agree that the news is terrible — but agency reporting in general.

This doesn't just cover PPC agencies, but also SEO agencies, email marketing agencies, PR agencies, or any sort of agency that has ongoing monthly work and growth metrics to share.

When we started our agency, one of the first things we noticed was the quality of monthly reports that we were seeing from other agencies. Usually, when we inherit accounts, we like to see past performance reports in order to establish a baseline for the future. When clients would send their old reports, we weren't really impressed. Very few agencies did it well.

In most cases, reports were just screenshots of Google Analytics copied and pasted into a Word doc. Or reports were generated by one of those automated reporting services that integrate with Google Ads or Search Console.

Numbers are important. But more important is the *truth*.

See, anyone can send over a spreadsheet of numbers. Anyone can screenshot a view within Google Analytics. But numbers without the proper context and story are literally irrelevant. Nobody knows what they're looking at when you send over a spreadsheet with 25 columns and multiple sheets and 300 rows of transaction data. It's a mess.

Instead, consistency and context are massively valuable.

Discarding the irrelevant noise is even *more* valuable.

What we decided to do is create extremely detailed reports that present our paid search approach in plain-English context.

Clients rarely care about specific metrics, at the end of the day. They want to know they have a profitable ROI, and they want to know their "big goals" are met. Figuring out their big goals, and presenting the metrics that matter the most to achieving their big goals, and explaining in non-technical jargon how you're going about this process, will create the most appreciated monthly report you'll ever send.

Once we started creating these reports, we found that clients really loved them. We explained exactly what we were doing, we explained numerical results in straightforward text, and included plenty of visual graphs and screenshots of ads, placements, and results over time.

Our simple, 4-page reports gave more actual data and insight than the 50-page cluttered reports that other agencies had sent.

Eventually, Google Data Studio came onto the scene and as it grew in functionality, we converted to using it for our reports. Easy integration with different channels enabled us to create customized reporting, while also being able to include our plain-English descriptions.

GOOGLE DATA STUDIO & THE POWER OF LIVE DASHBOARDS

The state of agency reporting, as I mentioned, is dismal. Yet it is so important to clients, even if they don't always know it.

Your clients are busy. They have a business to run. Most of them don't want to waste time looking at reports.

Give them about 3 critical numbers to look at. Numbers you can consistently report on, month over month, that are tied directly to their bottom line.

Usually, these numbers are very simple. For PPC agencies, these numbers might be cost per acquisition, cost per click, or ROAS (return on ad spend). For SEO agencies, these numbers might include organic traffic volume, amount of sales attributed to organic traffic, or brand search volume. For email marketing agencies, this could mean gross number of emails sent, open rates, click rates, amount of unsubscribes, and conversions tied directly to emails.

The great benefit of using something like Data Studio is that you can create a custom dashboard, link it up to the appropriate data sources (Google Ads, Analytics, Search Console, Shopify, WooCommerce, etc) and have an automatically updated dashboard that lets your clients see results in almost real time.

This can free up time for you to engage in monthly overview calls, thinking more about ten-thousand-foot strategies and long-term goals rather than dealing with small things like how much cost per click increased this week.

SEE REPORTS THROUGH THE EYES OF THE CLIENT

Reporting is critical. But often, I've noticed that in search marketing world, we can easily become myopic and forget to see performance through the eyes of the most important person: the client.

If you've been staring at the Google Ads interface for hours, it's pretty easy to focus on phrase match or tCPA or linear attribution or Quality Score or CPC and forget what matters most: that the client is fulfilling their goals.

This should inform the way we craft our reporting. Too often we cram our reports full of metrics that no client actually gives a crap about. Most good clients don't care about these metrics. They want us to do our job, and they want us to tell them how to make more money. Simple as that.

Looking at some of these old reports, I was simply flabbergasted at the messiness of them. If *we* couldn't even interpret them, after years of analytics experience, how could you expect a client to interpret this endless spreadsheet of intimidating, mostly meaningless numbers?

That's why we made a conscious effort at Discosloth to craft reports that are client-focused. We focus more on explaining details in plain English, along with the metrics that are direct goals for the clients.

It's always helpful to take a step back and consider why we

even exist, as agencies, anyway. We exist to help clients do things they don't want to — or *can't* — do. And most of the time, that's making money via marketing. As long as we can speak in their language, the language of revenue and bottom lines and expenses, we'll be doing both them and ourselves a service.

Chapter Takeaways

1. What quantifiable elements of your job can you communicate in your reporting?

2. How often, and how detailed, do your reports need to be?

3. What elements of your work can be tracked and analyzed?

4. What main metric do your clients use to quantify "success" with your projects?

PRICING & BILLING

"When somebody says it's not about the money, it's about the money." - H.L. Mencken[12]

One of the most common questions I get from freelancers, and would-be agency founders, is how to set pricing.

There is an endless range of pricing models, and to be fair, there's not really any single "right" way to price your work. Often, the best pricing model depends upon so many other factors: what kind of work you're doing, what sort of clients you're going after, whether your agency business model is low-volume or high-volume, or what sort of overhead you're working with.

As a freelancer, I played with many sorts of different pricing models, but in general it was project-based (I was a creative, so projects were one-off opportunities which usually lasted several

---

[12] Every once in a while, I'll come across a fellow who asks me about starting an agency. And he'll say stuff about wanting to help people grow, or wanting to create an agency that charges fair prices, or wants to build a socially responsible agency. That's all fair and good. Then I remember this Mencken quote.

weeks or months).

When we started our agency, we went with the model that was, at the time, the most common pricing model for paid search agencies. This model (percentage of ad spend) was a holdover from traditional media-buying agencies, and was the most popular form of structuring pricing within the PPC world for a long time. Eventually, we determined that this was an especially confusing and poor pricing model which disincentivized our clients from spending the amount on advertising which was best for their return on investment.

We shifted to a flat fee, monthly retainer model. This had multiple benefits for us: not only could we easily predict cash flow, but we could bill up front, build in necessary margins, and scale even with smaller clients. It was also a massive benefit for onboarding clients. We discovered that clients really liked knowing what they were going to pay us each month, and not feeling like we had some sort of profit incentive for making their ad accounts spend more than necessary.

Many agencies are going towards the retainer model, so it's gaining in popularity these days. Others still do some sort of hybrid model (base fee + ad spend) and even others charge hourly. None of these are wrong choices, necessarily, but I do think there are benefits and downsides to all of them.

FEE MODELS

The first fee model — and one that I try to actively discourage every time I consult with a freelancer or agency owner who is struggling with revenue — is the hourly model.

There is a simple reason for this. There are only so many hours in the week. Hourly pricing not only caps your possible revenue, but it also requires you to actually spend lots of time on things. The incentive is perverse, in my mind. Not only does it encourage you, the agency, to spend too much time on things, but it means that your client usually doesn't want you to spend too much time on things (if it costs them money). And in order to get your income up to a respectable level (and scale past that, if possible) it means that your hourly fee must equal that of a plumber or doctor. No client wants to look at your invoice and see that their 30-minute phone call cost them $300. The rare exclusion is for consulting, especially if it is business or brand focused.

For consulting, however, I suggest a modification of hourly pricing. Since there is rarely a deliverable in consulting (usually it's just your time and expertise that's needed, not actual execution) you are still selling "time" in a sense. I think day rates are usually more practical in this case. Instead of pricing your marketing consulting at $100/hour, it's usually better and easier to give a client a day rate (and charge half days if necessary). This way, you can filter out serious consulting opportunities and offer more value for a chunk. I would rather make $1,000/day for consulting, than charge ten separate hours at $100/each.

Some agencies use a performance-based fee. This is typically charging a percentage of revenue, or some form of commission from leads or sales provided. There isn't anything especially wrong with this model, but in practice I have rarely seen it used by a professional, sustainable agency. For whatever reason, this sort of pricing is almost exclusively used by somewhat questionable agencies, the sort of folks that run call centers getting Medicare helpline leads from seniors or selling grey-market pharmaceutical products. Now, that may sound biased of me, and perhaps it is, but there's a reason that most professional agencies won't use this model. It's mostly because not everything is within the agency's control. Agencies don't want to be held responsible for the client's customer service, pricing, technical issues, and internal problems. If you are to structure your pricing on a commission basis, you need full access to the client's accounting, CRM, tracking, and analytics in order to properly attribute the leads and value you're providing.

For many years, the most common pricing model for PPC agencies was percentage of ad spend. Typically, agencies would charge between 10-20% of total ad spend as their fee. However, this model only works with digital agencies who are directly selling ads (it isn't applicable for agencies who build websites, do graphic design, or doing SEO). Since this was the industry norm when we started Discosloth, that's what we did as well. Moving away from this model was the absolute best thing we did for our top line. Similar to hourly billing, I find that the incentive can be perverse. It creates a bias for the agency to convince clients to spend more on ads, even when it may not be in the client's best interest. It also makes the client unwilling to spend more on ads even when spending more *is* in their best interest.

Project-based pricing is good for certain work at certain agencies (and is the *only* reasonable option for many) especially when there are concrete deliverables and when most work is one-off opportunities, like building websites or designing a logo. Although project-based revenue is a slim line in our financial pie chart, we use this model from time to time when we do one-off account audits, or campaign setups without management.

The final model (and a model which works well in many different types of agencies, not just advertising-centric agencies) is the flat fee or retainer model. This is the model we landed on at Discosloth. Simply put, we come up with a flat monthly price that makes us money and is achievable for the client, and we start working for them. Typically this fee does end up being somewhere in the same range as a percentage-based fee would be, but it's more coincidental than anything else (we still have to compete in the general cost range of our competition, and there is a vague correlation between ad spend and campaign complexity). The benefits of this model are multiple.

First, it's simple. Keeping things simple is crucial to scaling an agency — it's one of our core principles — and at the end of the day it allows us to make far more revenue than if we made things more complex. Second, it allows us to charge up-front. We prefer to charge monthly, getting paid at the beginning of the month, as this improves our cashflow, lessens financial liability, and gives us the ability to make quick decisions for our future. And third, it's scalable and just far more profitable in all manner of speaking. When we start reaching capacity, we simply raise our fees for all new clients. After a year or so, once we've lost some of our older clients and are assessing new leads, or perhaps after we've made a specialist hire and can accommodate a few more accounts, we start reaching a new level of capacity...and we simply raise our fees once again. We put a healthy amount of margin into all of our fees, even our small business tier.

GROWING YOUR FEES

As we covered in the previous section, we work on a flat fee-based model. If we want to start making more money, we don't have to increase our percentage of ad spend, or spend more hours working. We just raise our retainer. Clients become higher quality. We can do better work with better clients. Everyone makes more money. End of story.

To date, after five years of running Discosloth and working with hundreds of clients, we have never once increased our rates. We have grandfathered everyone into our pricing, and we only increase prices on new clients that we onboard.

Lately, with inflationary pressures on the economy, a lot of agency folks have been increasing their fees. I don't blame them, and we may have to do that in the future. I think it will be fine, since folks running businesses are experiencing inflation themselves and understand the need to preserve margins. We *could* have increased prices for existing customers several times, but we've just chosen not to.

The good news is, as long as you are onboarding a steady stream of new clients, even as seldom as once every month or two, you can adjust your pricing as you go.

The golden rule of pricing and growing fees — which we've

tried to live by at Discosloth — is that *if you're too busy, your prices are too low*.

Every time we find ourselves maxed out to capacity, without much bandwidth to take on new clients, it's time to increase our pricing.

It's a delicate balance between having work and making more money. You want both, but you can't just jump into the deep "making more money" end of the pool without first wading through the shallow "having work" end.

Sometimes, you just have to have work. At at the beginning of your agency path, *any* work is better than none at all, even if the pricing isn't where you want it to be.

There's some ingrained resistance to this idea among a lot of new agency founders, and I've had some puzzling and frustrating conversations with folks about this. It almost always comes from a place of inexperience, so it's worth explaining the thought process.

Most folks reach out to me coming from a place of genuine curiosity and desire to learn. I had one fellow email me, however, who was absolutely fixated in his own version of agency reality. It was almost impossible to get him to shift from his initial mindset.

"Managing an ad account for less than $500-600 a month or less does not seem appealing to me, would prefer to make at least $1k," the fellow wrote.

"That's entirely up to you," I wrote back, "and depends on your overhead. If you can get a lot of clients paying $1k+ then that's great. However, at first cash flow is most important. We took on a lot of lower paying clients the first few years until we were able to slowly increase our average revenue per client."

"Any lower," he wrote, "and it starts to feel like I would rather not put in as much work as I normally would."

It clicked for me. He was coming from a salaried employee, biweekly paycheck perspective. He simply did not understand scale. When you get a paycheck every month, it's easy to think in terms of 1 x $6,000 instead of 10 x $600.

"That's entirely up to you on how much you are motivated to work," I responded, "but it's more about stability and scaling rather than individual accounts. In my opinion it's more important to be at capacity than to lose out on revenue because pricing is too high."

He responded by saying his hourly rate was higher than that, and he couldn't take a pay cut from his existing job simply to on-board cheap clients.

I tried explaining that it's extremely hard to just start up your agency and magically onboard a half-dozen clients that pay $1000 a month. And if you're hung up on what hourly rate you're "worth" or the minimum amount you need to take home each month, you're going to end up losing a lot of $600 clients while caught up in a desperate grab for $1000 clients.

And the reality is: if you miss out on a few of those $600 clients, fast forward a few years and you'll miss out on a few of those $6,000 clients.

INVOICING & BILLING

There are lots of ways to get paid — and you should consider supporting them all. Two methods, however, stand above all the rest.

Accepting credit card payments is critical for our cashflow. Before we started accepting credit cards, our average time to payment (from sending out an invoice to getting the payment) was almost two weeks. When we shifted to credit cards, our average time to payment reduced to 3 days.

After a year or two, we decided to push the envelope even further. We were already pivoting away from the percentage of ad spend model, and since we now had a flat fee retainer model in place, we had the ability to automate our invoicing. For many of our clients, their credit cards are automatically invoiced every month. Time to payment is immediate!

Quite a few invoicing and merchant services support this model (we use Wave, but other common providers are Stripe or Square).

The downside of credit card payments is the payment processing fee, which is usually around 3%. This may not seem like a lot, but start billing a few hundred thousand bucks a year, and those fees start adding up. We are fine with these fees, especially for smaller accounts. The cashflow benefits and peace of mind from immediate payment are worth 3%.

However, with larger clients, we typically accept ACH (which, in the US at least, is very important) or even paper checks. We typically do this with long-term trusted clients, and the benefit is that there is no transaction fee.

We had some unpleasant experiences at the beginning of our agency's life, one in particular in which a partner agency went bot-

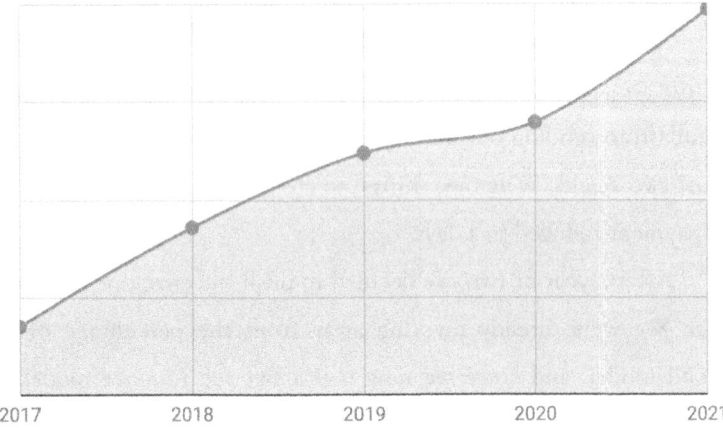

This is our YoY (year-over-year) agency revenue growth. Our first year, 2017, was really only around 8 months of operation, so it is especially low in comparison to the following years. The interesting part about this graph is that, since the end of 2017, we have always had roughly the same number of clients on retainer (averaging between 20 and 30 per month). Our fees have grown, yet our service range has narrowed. We saw a slowdown in growth temporarily in 2020, due to the various lockdowns and mandates which negatively affected several of our clients.

tom-up and defaulted on what was a very high payment at the time for us. Since they were located in Australia, it was almost impossible to recover during their bankruptcy process, so we chalked that one up to a lesson learned the hard way.

Since then, we charge upfront, and it's served us well. We don't start work on a new campaign with a new client until we've been paid, which sets a standard for both us and the client. It's been a good decision for us, and I recommend that any micro-agency adopt a similar policy.

Chapter Takeaways

....

1. Are you in this to make money?

2. How *much* money do you want to make?

3. Early in the life of your agency, you can't charge as much as you will be able to later on. How do you plan on increasing your pricing?

4. How can you convert most of your revenue into recurring income, rather than one-off income?

5. Which pricing model is most attractive to you? Hourly, performance-based, flat fee/retainer, or percentage of ad spend? Any other hybrid models that seem attractive?

6. Would you want to charge up front, upon completion, or a mixture of the two?

7. How soon after invoicing would you expect to be paid?

SCALING YOUR AGENCY

"Only the Americans could afford it." — Kazuo Ishiguro[13]

Which is more important at the end of the day: having higher overall revenue, or bringing more income home?

To frame it another way: would you rather own an agency with two million dollars in revenue and twenty employees, where your take-home profit is $150k, or would you rather own an agency making half a million in revenue with three employees, where your take-home profit is $300k?

Seems like a no-brainer to me. I'll take the second option any day. Leaner, easier, more efficient, and far more profitable.

However, some folks would rather take less profit home, but have the larger-sized agency.

Our model for scaling an agency is not by scaling head count, but by scaling revenue instead.

The key to keeping head count (and expenses) low, which in turn increases how much you can take home at the end of the year,

---

[13] Kazuo Ishiguro, *The Remains of the Day*

is by narrowing down the services you offer until only the most profitable remain. It can be difficult "pruning" your services away, since you are likely getting a bit of revenue from all of them, but it's worth looking at them and analyzing if they are truly bringing you the most profit. Is it worth offering graphic design as an add-on service, if it means you have to have an extra full-time staff member on payroll? Is it worth offering SEO as a service, if you keep running into project problems and it ends up taking a lot of meeting time? Is it worth doing paid search, if it's not your primary expertise and you're having to spend a lot of time and money educating yourself and your team on it?

These are all decisions unique to your agency, but crucial to making income-based decisions rather than revenue-based decisions.

ONE-OFF PROJECTS OR ONGOING WORK?

Earlier in the book, we went over possible technical verticals that an agency can explore. I definitely have my biases as to which of these are more profitable or scalable, but the reality is that wild success can be had in any of these.

I think there is a further way to split these verticals, however, and it's one of my favorite ways to divide up agencies. there are one-off work agencies, which are project-based, and there are ongoing work agencies, which are more focused on monthly, continuous work.

A project-based agency would be best represented by a web design or branding agency. Typically, these agencies get major one-time projects, like a website redesign, or an e-commerce store development project, or a logo redesign, or an entire brand development project. That's not to say that these agencies *can't* develop ongoing income. Many web design agencies have developed some level of ongoing income (either by selling hosting, or maintenance contracts, or by creating digital products/SaaS products that generate some residual revenue for the agency). It's just very hard for project-based agencies to develop a sustainable monthly revenue base that can be forecast or projected into the future.

An ongoing-work agency is typically a PPC, SEO, or other "performance marketing" sort of agency, which provides continuous monthly services over the course of a long period of time — managing paid search campaigns or SEO campaigns or email campaigns. That's not to say that ongoing-work agencies can't do one-off projects, either. Often a PPC agency can sell a one-off audit, or an SEO agency can do a one-time website migration.

There are a few sorts of technical verticals which are in the middle of ongoing and one-off. These agencies are UI/UX agencies (sometimes this is one-time work on new website launches, but it can also include ongoing website maintenance and optimization for larger clients) or often copywriting agencies. In most cases, copywriting projects are one-off, but larger clients can retain copywriting agencies for ongoing work as well.

I'm biased in my assessment of ongoing versus one-off work, so it's probably a good time to once again remind my readers that *our way is not the only way*. There are many agencies out there who are wildly successful and do it absolutely different than we do.

Here's why I prefer ongoing work: pace, cash flow, and scalability.

Pace. It's important to us at Discosloth because of what we want. We do our best work when we're focusing on the *work* rather than constantly trying to get more clients. We want clients who will work with us every month for the next four or five years. We would rather make a little bit every month, rather than a whole lot once a year. This allows us to develop lasting relationships with our clients, get to know their industries intimately, and have massive positive effects on their ROI over the course of months or even years.

Cash flow. This, and this alone, has been the primary driving factor in our growth and sustainability as an agency. We can predict our revenue for months in advance. We know what we'll make next month before we make it. This lets us build in a healthy margin, pay our expenses and payroll, and in the case of unexpected situations, we have weeks to figure out what we need to do next.

Scalability. With pace and cash flow, comes scalability. When we are profitable, and when we have bandwidth, we can make better long-term decisions. We can look at our workload, our profit margins, and decide if we need to hire next quarter, how much we can budget for our annual company retreat, or decide if we have some extra money to spend on bonuses or more dividends for ourselves, or if we need to cut back on expenses over the summer. It keeps us in the black, thinking ahead, and moving forward.

We have definitely taken on some one-off projects, but we do not build those into our revenue expectations. We consider those one-off projects to be occasional gravy.

At Discosloth, we would *much* rather make a thousand dollars a month for a year, rather than $12,000 one-time (although early in your newborn agency's life, though, that one-time $12,000 would be hard to pass up).

We have gone through months of less revenue (especially once or twice when we have lost a "whale" client) but we have not lost money in a single month. That's because we take such a paced, forward-looking approach to our cash flow. Lose a client? It's okay, because we have twenty other clients on retainer this month.

Project-based agencies can sometimes fall into a cash flow trap, because even after months or years of consistent revenue, a dry spell can literally sink the whole agency. It's always important to have a cash buffer, but even the most well-funded agency will find it difficult to survive months of unknown revenue.

Getting clients is hard, no question about it. But onboarding a one-time customer is *harder* than onboarding a customer who pays you monthly. Why?

It's harder to convince someone to pay you $12,000 all at once, rather than $1,000 a month for a year. It's harder to find the same volume of clients for sustainable projects and cash flow...will you be able to convince someone new to pay you $12,000 *every* month? It's just much easier to find 12 clients to pay you $1,000 monthly for a year, rather than find 12 clients to pay you $12,000 once.

Some of this is because it's more iterative. Wouldn't you rather have a *few* $1,000 clients giving you at least some revenue while you add to your retainer base, rather than perhaps going a couple months without anything, while you hunt for the $12,000 paydays?

Of course, I'm grossly simplifying the process, and it's far more subtle than I'm explaining. Many development agencies do extremely well. I just don't think that's the way to develop a truly profitable and sustainable micro-agency, which after all, is what this book is all about.

Our approach is all about simplicity, sustainability, stability, and profit margin. I think we've dialed our own approach in quite well. Because of this experience, I think that project-based agencies would do well to explore creating some ongoing revenue streams for themselves.

PROFIT MARGIN

I know quite a few agency owners, and after having dozens of conversations with them over the years, I've been able to identify which ones are making bank, and which ones are barely holding on. The results are always surprising, at least looking from the outside.

I know one fellow who runs a fairly well-known agency within our niche. I think most people would assume that this agency is absolutely rolling in the dough. He provides three or four core services, and has cumulative thousands of followers both on social platforms and on the speaking circuit. He's quite open about his revenue. His agency did a little under $600,000 last year.

Unfortunately, his financial reality is a little different. However, he admits he has months where he *loses* money. Let's do some arithmetic.

He is bringing in an average of $50,000 per month. Yet, since he's losing money some months, that means his overhead is more than that. I'd assume a lot of that comes from too many staff on payroll - a half-dozen at last count, all of which are living in an extremely high cost of living area. Even if he's only paying his six staff members $5,000/mo (and that is likely on the low side) that means his payroll costs alone would be $30,000/mo. Not a whole lot of space left for either his own profit ...or wiggle room for bad months. That's why he loses money some months.

Just looking from the outside, I think that the answer is pretty clear. He scaled too fast. In order to achieve that top line revenue number, he started offering more services. Too many services, none of which were primary revenue drivers, in which he had to onboard some full-time, in-house staff. I suspect he could have only hired 2-3 staff, stuck with the single service that provides him with the most margin, and ended up with double the amount of profit that he takes home now.

Lower volume...but higher margins.

This may sound like I'm contradicting myself. Earlier, I said that you should accept more clients paying less, rather than a few paying more. And now I'm saying that you need less with higher margin. Make up your mind! What's up with this?

The reality is that both are true. You just need to find your perfect balance.

In our case, we know we work best with around 20-24 clients at a time. This is our max for being productive, having enough time to spend working on each campaign, and still have a diversification of clients large enough that if we lose a few clients, we are still doing fine financially.

WHALES

Having a distributed source of revenue matters.

When I was in college, I interned for an agency that produced campaigns for a very, very large client. This agency referred to this client as their "whale". The contract had been ongoing for a couple decades, at least since the mid 1990s, and was worth several million dollars in revenue per year.

Shortly after my internship ended, so did the contract.

The agency, which employed nearly forty people, had to close their doors.

In their benefit, they did so in the most gracious way possible. They had no debt. They sold off their very expensive studio and cinema cameras. They gave everyone a nice severance. And the owners retired with a nice savings account, and opened a little bakery.

It's hard to call this agency's closure a mistake. It was a successful run and it provided a great career for dozens of people, and made the owners wealthy. But the writing was on the wall: they had a whale, and only a whale.

Perhaps it's just because it was my first exposure to agency business, but this has stuck with me over the years. I've always been cautious (some could say paranoid) about Discosloth depending too greatly upon a single whale.

Instead, drawing upon my laconic Southern charm, I like to say that we've got to run on mashed potatoes, and the whales are gravy. For those who didn't grow up in the sultry humid summers of

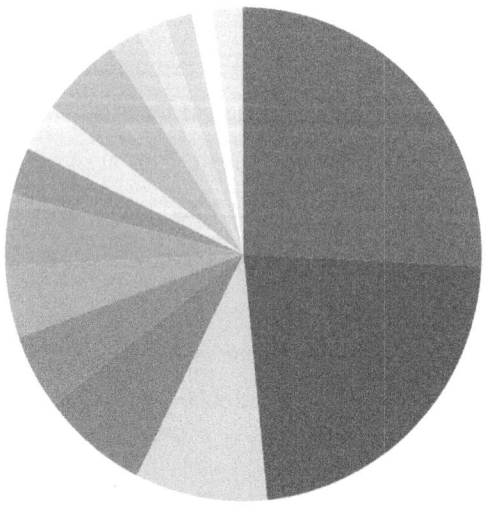

Discosloth's 2021 revenue per client. This does not include one-off work or short term (less than 3 month) clients.

Arkansas, that essentially means that Discosloth keeps enough diversification of revenue in smaller clients. We keep our margins high enough, expenses low enough, and enough smaller clients on retainer, so that even if we lose our whales, we're still making money.

As of 2022, we have two long-term "whale" clients. Together, these two clients make up nearly 50% of our revenue. Losing one or both of our whale clients would hurt, but we sleep easy at night knowing that, even if worst comes to worst, we'll be able to lose both of these clients and still be able to stay profitable.

I like to keep our portfolio of clients balanced in terms of account size, simply because I see value in having both large clients (for revenue) and in small clients (for stability). From the graph, you'll notice that nearly 10 of our smaller clients barely provide us with the same revenue as a single "whale" client, and each of those smaller clients is definitely still a lot of work, but there's a reasoning behind this.

A single client can leave us at any time. It would be very, very strange if all 10 of our smallest clients wanted to leave us at the same time.

Increasingly, as we move upmarket, our "small" clients become bigger clients. That's why you see a healthy mid-range in our graph, which are mostly all newer clients we've onboarded recently with slightly higher pricing (to this day, we have never raised prices on an existing client...we just grandfather people in).

THE 5-50 VALLEY OF DEATH

In the world of 3D animation, there is a term called the uncanny valley. This is the phrase used when characters are *almost* realistic. It's when everything looks almost real but not quite...there's something off, like the eyes are dead, or the facial expressions are strange. The uncanny valley didn't exist in the 80s and 90s, back when 3D animation was extremely crude. Nothing was realistic enough to convince anybody, so it didn't bother folks. The uncanny valley only appeared when animation became *almost* perfect.

A similar valley exists in the world of digital agencies, but it exists in the form of reduced profitability that comes along with a certain agency size. When an agency is very small (say 3-5 employees) it can be extremely profitable. Likewise, when an agency is very large (say 50+ employees) it can also be extremely profitable. It's the middle ground that I like to call the 5-50 Valley of Death...where you have increased expenditures but not necessarily proportionally increased revenue.

It *looks* good but it isn't *quite* good.

All of the large agencies that exist had to push through this valley. Sometimes they lost money during this phase. Other times they simply scaled well.

Here is the great secret about micro-agencies: you can make more profit with a small-sized agency than with a medium-sized agency. And with significantly less headache.

There isn't anything wrong with wanting to build a large agency — but I don't know anything about that, and this book is about micro-agencies.

Once your agency starts getting into the double digits when it comes to head count, your overhead expenses start really piling up. You need more office space, equipment, HR, and probably need to weight your staff towards account management/sales rather than fulfillment (because you've got to keep your bucket of leads full in order to pay all those employees). As an owner, it's one thing to bring home a lot of money at the end of the year when you just have two or three employees to take care of. It can be easy to cover generous salaries, and be extremely picky about who is on your team. It's another thing to offer the same generous salaries and benefits to a dozen folks, and expect to be able to also bring home the same amount of profit. Agencies and finances, it turns out, don't really scale linearly.

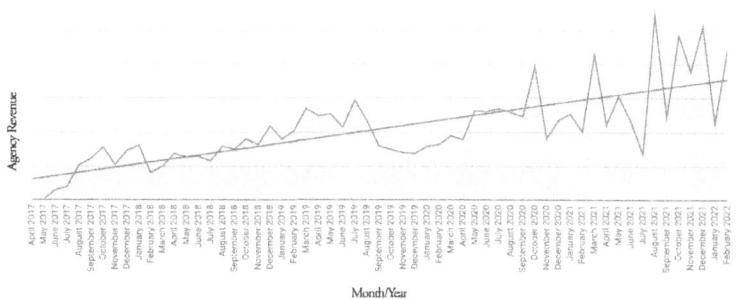

This is our agency revenue each month, starting in April 2017, along with a linear trendline. It's worth noting that, although you can't exactly see it on the graph, we were profitable in our first month: $4, specifically.

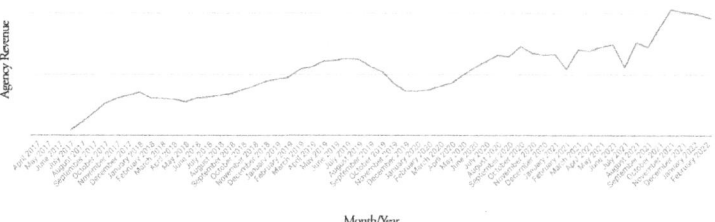

This is the same chart, smoothed and given a 4-month running average. Since our monthly revenue can vary drastically (some clients paying late, losing a large client, gaining several large clients) this can help visualize the growth more realistically. You'll notice the up-and-downs near the end. This isn't churn as much as incoming client payments coming in twice in some months, and skipping the next.

Chapter Takeaways

1. Would you prefer one-off projects, or ongoing work?

2. After you've read some of our examples and case studies, do you think your agency would be best at specializing in a technical niche (for example, SEO for Shopify stores) or an industry vertical (for example, ecommerce for hunting retailers)?

3. Are you the type of person who prefers complex solutions with lots of tools and processes, or a minimalistic, simple approach?

THE RECIPE

As we mentioned in the very first pages of this book, there is more than one way to build a successful agency.

But I think there is a handful of factors, all of which we've covered in this book, which are extremely conducive to the sort of agency I want to run: a small, simple, profitable, and sustainable micro-agency doing great work.

We covered these factors early on, but it's worth taking a look at once again, after having read the background of how we came to these conclusions. Here are the factors...the ingredients to the Discosloth recipe, so to speak:

1. Specialization
2. Simplicity
3. Brand
4. Cashflow/Profit
5. Revenue Adjacency

I'll take a few brief paragraphs for each of these, one more time. It can't hurt, because I think these are the most critical elements to a micro-agency's success.

Specialization can take the form of industry vertical or technical niche. This means you can either specialize in serving certain industries, or you can specialize in offering a specific technical service. The benefits of specialization are that you can be far more efficient, spend far less time, and develop a reputation in your niche far, far easier.

Simplicity means focusing on the most effective areas of your business, and discarding the rest. It means doubling down on what you do best, and doing more of it. Cut extraneous meetings. Remove distracting processes. Don't use too many tools. Don't waste time. Focus on doing good work, and keep it simple for everyone on your team. This results in lower overhead, more attention on your real actual work, and ultimately higher margins.

Brand is the image your agency projects into the industry. When you build a brand which accurately reflects who *you* are... people will flock to that. You will start getting inbound leads rather than having to go out and look for work. You will generate content and authority in your space, which means people will start coming to you for a solution. This means you can charge higher prices and be pickier about the sort of work you do.

Cashflow is critical, and the most often misunderstood by agency founders. Having more money coming in than is going out (every single month) is the only bulletproof means to ensure that your agency won't go bottom up the first time you lose a whale client, or the economy collapses, or some black swan event happens. Keeping a steady stream of monthly revenue coming in, and making sure it's way more than you need, is the only way to survive long-term without needless stress.

Revenue adjacency means finding a niche where you're connected to the client's bottom line. There's a reason, as we covered in early chapters, that sales guys make a lot more money than creative guys. It's not necessarily because creativity isn't important, but it's because sales guys have careers that are tied directly to the company numbers. Marketing can be tied to company success as well — and that's where analytics and attribution come in. The more that you can prove you *do* for the client, the more you can charge and the longer your clients will stick around.

These factors may seem simple. And they are.

But you might be surprised at how often agency owners do the exact opposite of these factors. Instead of developing specialization, simplicity and efficiency, a good brand, positive cashflow, and being revenue adjacent, they go to the polar south: generalization, complexity, no brand, negative cashflow or low margins, and not tying the success of their agency to their client's revenue stream.

AFTERWORD

A common trope you'll often hear in the marketing world is "there are no mistakes, only lessons to be learned."

To a degree, that quote is an element of truth, but it's not quite as simple as that.

There are some mistakes you do *not* want to make. There are some mistakes that will sink you financially. Some mistakes are far worse than others!

Starting our agency was one of the best professional decisions of our lives. The path from the beginning to the present wasn't easy, and we made plenty of mistakes and missteps on the way. But looking back, I don't think I would actually want to change our path. Although we learned many things the hard way, we cultivated a certain approach and ethos to managing an agency that prevented us from making those fatal mistakes that cannot be backtracked or erased.

I've seen many folks go out on their own, and the cold hard truth is that not everybody can make it work. Many folks do extremely well at starting up an agency. I have seen folks thrive beyond belief while doing work they truly enjoy. I have also seen other folks, unfortunately, make some critical mistakes that have wiped them out in both emotional and financial aspects.

I think it is a disservice to blindly encourage everyone to start an agency. The world is rarely black and white, and not everyone is suited for it (or even *wants* to). There is a level of security in full-time employment that simply can't be universally replicated by agency ownership.

However, if you're thinking of going out on your own, and are keeping your eyes wide open to the potential benefits *and* potential downsides of starting a small business, it is our hope that this book will help you avoid some of the critical mistakes that many folks make, and also help you identify some of the important decisions that should be made in order to foster success.

Our approach has been a blend of a safe, conservative perspective (no debt, slow yet steady growth, and a deep focus on specific niches) and an unsafe, progressive perspective (bold branding, lots of confidence, and some quite unorthodox opinions within our field).

At the same time, I wouldn't ever want to encourage someone to *not* start an agency. Despite a constant stream of folks proclaiming that marketing is dead, or even prophesying the imminent demise of certain channels like email marketing or website design or digital advertising, it somehow keeps on ticking.

When we started Discosloth, we gave it five years before the landscape completely changed, and we'd have to pivot away from search advertising (disregard why we started an agency when we thought the field might disappear within five years).

Five years later, we are happy to have been proven very wrong.

There's never a better time to start than now!

Additional Resources

The books in this section may not be highly relevant to your specific quest, as our own niche is in paid search/pay-per-click advertising. However, at the very least these resources will serve as great examples of what we've done with content creation & branding during the first 5 years of creating our micro-agency. Spending time developing these resources worked well for us, and I think that building similar resources in your own niche will work well for you.

Becoming A Digital Marketer: Gaining the Hard & Soft Skills for a Tech-Driven Marketing Career

Our first book was oriented towards the absolute beginning digital marketer: students, or people who want to switch careers into an entry-level digital marketing role. This book has done quite well, becoming an Amazon bestseller in its category and selling almost 4,000 copies since its publication in 2019. This book has been adopted into the curriculum of several dozen universities, including University of Texas, Gonzaga, Franklin & Marshall, West Virginia University, University of Southern Maine, and others.

The Beginner's Guide to Google Ads: A Short Guide For Creating Successful PPC Campaigns

Anya's short guide to PPC was developed and expanded from our online guide which we launched for free. Since publication, we have published this book in France through Les Éditions Eyrolles, in partnership with Ad's Up Consulting (one of the largest French PPC agencies). You can find the shorter, totally free online English version of this book on our website at discosloth.com/beginners-guide-to-ppc

Making Remote Work Work: How To Work Remotely & Build Teams From Anywhere In The World

This book is a brief overview of how to make remote work functional within a small team, most importantly learning how to work asynchronously and triage your internal communications in a way that makes sense.

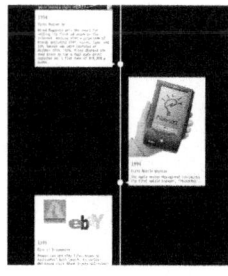

A Visual Timeline of Digital Marketing

We published this tongue-in-cheek fun microsite on the Discosloth website several years ago, covering internet advertising trivia from the invention of email to the current day. Surprisingly, this is a popular microsite that brings us quite a bit of organic traffic. You can find this at discosloth.com/visual-timeline-of-digital-marketing

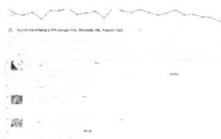

r/SearchAdvertising

Starting a subreddit dedicated to search advertising (our specific technical niche) and agency growth/business in general was one of the best ideas we've had recently. We spend countless hours contributing to subreddits like this, freely engaging and educating folks of all skillsets and experience levels. You can find this subreddit at reddit.com/r/SearchAdvertising

Printed in Great Britain
by Amazon

22345592R00088